THE SONG REPERTOIRE
OF
AMELIA AND JANE HARRIS

The
Scottish Text Society

27 George Square, Edinburgh EH8 9LD, Scotland

THE SONG REPERTOIRE
OF
AMELIA AND JANE HARRIS

Edited by

Emily Lyle
Kaye McAlpine
Anne Dhu McLucas

THE SCOTTISH TEXT SOCIETY

2002

27 George Square
Edinburgh EH8 9LD
Scotland

ISBN 1 897976 17 8

Printed by Antony Rowe Ltd,
Chippenham, Wiltshire, England

CONTENTS

PREFACE

We are pleased to present this work by two sisters living in Scotland in the latter part of the nineteenth century who were not only aware of their heritage of song, as many women must have been before them, but were confident enough to make a written collection of their family songs not for their own use but for the world at large. Even with the degree of confidence they exhibited, however, Amelia and Jane Harris required male intermediaries, and they sought out distinguished professors of English to act for them in making their songs known. However, since the professor to whom the first manuscript was sent, W. E. Aytoun, died prematurely without publishing anything from it, and since the recipient of the second manuscript, Francis James Child, scattered items from the collection through the volumes of his extensive work, it is only with the present edition that we can see this repertoire as a rounded whole and appreciate its place in the Scottish song tradition. The fact that the collection was put together *twice* is a bonus, for it means that this edition can be drawn upon not only for the songs in themselves, but also for the contribution the different versions offer to the debate on what exactly is involved in receiving and passing on an oral heritage, a debate that has centred in ballad studies in the past on the versions of Mrs Brown of Falkland (see D. Buchan 1972, Anderson and Pettitt 1979 and Henderson 1980). Comparison of the different Harris versions written down with an interval of about fourteen years between them was only made possible through the exciting rediscovery of the first manuscript (which had been lost for many years) by Mr Hilary Corke in 1955. We are extremely grateful to Mr Corke and his family for allowing the use of this manuscript (A) and for encouraging the publication of this volume. Material from MS B and the *Harris Letters* is published by permission of the Houghton Library, Harvard University, and the two Peter Buchan texts in Appendix B from Additional MSS 29408 ff. 123-5 by courtesy of the British Library.

We would like to thank the British Academy for making a grant in 1979 towards the cost of typing and Dr Ruth McQuillan and Peggy Morrison for preparing a typed and word-processed copy of the text. For advice on illustration and on the contents and layout of the volume, we would like to thank Dr Katherine Campbell, Professor Michael Chesnutt, Dr Rosalind K. Marshall and members of the Council and Editorial Committee of the Scottish Text Society. We are grateful to the librarians in Special Collections at the

University of Edinburgh (where MS A was made available for consultation) and in the Houghton Library, Harvard University. We would also like to express our appreciation to Hugh Amory for examining MS B and advising on its description, and to Robert Mathieson, Burial Ground Supervisor with City of Edinburgh Council, for helping in the location of the Harris sisters' burial plot in Warriston Cemetery.

This volume has been prepared for the press by Kaye McAlpine, who would like to thank Jason Hall for technical support through the process. Anne Dhu McLucas has been responsible for the editorial decisions on the music and for the music commentary in the notes as well as for the section on music in the introduction; she would like to thank William Campbell for preparing the computerised music samples and Morag MacLeod for her comments on the Gaelic air. Emily Lyle would like to express her appreciation to the School of Scottish Studies (now the Department of Celtic and Scottish Studies) at the University of Edinburgh for providing research facilities throughout the period she has worked on this project.

Finally, we would like to thank Dr Sally Mapstone, President of the Scottish Text Society, and Dr Nicola Royan, the society's Editorial Secretary, for facilitating the appearance of this volume. In association with its publication, a CD of the songs of Amelia and Jane Harris, sung by Katherine Campbell, is being released by Springthyme (Springthyme SPRCD 1041).

31 May 2002

Emily Lyle, Edinburgh
Kaye McAlpine, Edinburgh
Anne Dhu McLucas, Eugene, Oregon

ABBREVIATIONS

Child MSS: 33 vols.
Houghton Library, Harvard University, 25241.47*.

GD: *The Greig-Duncan Folk Song Collection* ed. P. Shuldham-Shaw, E. B. Lyle, et al. 8 vols. Aberdeen and Edinburgh 1981-2002.

Harris Letters: "Letters and papers relating to the Harris MS".
Houghton Library, Harvard University, 25241.41*.

MS A: "Old Scottish Ballads".
In the possession of Mrs Shirley Corke.

MS B: "Harris MS".
Houghton Library, Harvard University, 25241.17*.

TITLES

PART 1

SONGS APPEARING IN MS A WITH PARALLELS FROM MS B

PART 2

SONGS APPEARING ONLY IN MS B

ILLUSTRATIONS

Fig.1 William Edmonstoune Aytoun
(the recipient of MS A)

Fig. 2 Francis James Child
(the recipient of MS B)

INTRODUCTION

The manuscripts

The two manuscripts in this edition, which were written down by the sisters Amelia Harris (1815-1891) and Jane Harris (1823-1897), provide an important source for our knowledge of traditional Scottish song. They contain a family repertoire, mainly passed on orally to the sisters by their mother, Mrs David Harris, née Grace Dow, and also include some items taken down from others. The collection is unusual for the period in giving the music as well as the words of most of the songs. It is also unusual in providing, in many cases, two apparently independent records made with an interval of about fourteen years between them which means that the collection gives exceptional scope for the study of oral process.

Each of the two manuscripts was transmitted to a scholar with a passionate interest in ballads. The first one, MS A dated 1859, was sent to Professor William Edmonstoune Aytoun (1813-1865), Professor of Rhetoric and Belles Lettres at the University of Edinburgh and editor of *The Ballads of Scotland* (1858), and the second, MS B, was sent in 1873 to Professor Francis James Child (1825-1896), Boylston Professor of Rhetoric and Oratory at Harvard University, who was then at work on preparing his monumental edition of *The English and Scottish Popular Ballads* which was published in parts between 1882 and 1898.

Aytoun, besides being a professor at the University of Edinburgh, was sheriff of Orkney and Shetland, and his duties as sheriff took him to the Northern Isles. On one of these visits to the north he gave a lecture on ballads at Lerwick which was attended by Amelia Harris and the impression she received of him then encouraged her to send him her ballads and songs. In the following letter dated 12 November 1859 at Newburgh, Fife, and addressed to Professor Aytoun, University, Edinburgh, Amelia Harris gives an account of the collection she is sending by the same post.[1]

> Sir
>   I trust you will pardon me an entire stranger for addressing you, I think it is on a subject in w^h you take a lively interest.

---

[1] This letter is bound in at the beginning of MS A.

From my earliest recollection I have taken much pleasure in listening to old ballads and committing them to memory. – About a year ago it came into my mind to write down every scrap I remembered, along with the simple airs to w^h I had heard them sung – While so engaged, I observed both in the Scotch and American newspapers, notices of two vols. of Antient Ballads published by you – Three or four years ago I had the pleasure of hearing you lecture in Lerwick on Ancient Ballad poetry,[2] your appearance and lecture came vividly to my recollection, and it occurred to me, that I should forward my versions of Ballads to you, not that you might find many or any of them new to you, but they may be of interest to you in comparing with others, as they came down to me in a direct traditiGrey line. I learned the greater part of them from my mother, who would have been in her 80th year had she been alive.[3] She in her turn learned them in her early girlhood from a very old woman who was nurse in the family, and whose store was inexhaustible. I have been most scrupulous in writing them exactly as I heard them, leaving a blank, when I was in doubt as to a word or line. I may also add that I have *read* very few collections of Old Ballads, and that I was in the habit of dailly chaunting those sent, before I knew that the "Minstrelsy of the Scottish Borders" was in existence. No^s 27 & 28[4] I got from my father, who is now eighty five years of age[5] and whose first preceptor, a "Whittlegate Dominie," was an old man who had been servant to the Laird of Cluny and whose edition of the story was the same as that given in

---

[2] Two public lectures by "Sheriff Aytoun" on poetry and ballads, given in Kirkwall, Orkney, under the auspices of the Kirkwall Literary and Scientific Association, were reported in *The Orcadian* of 4 August 1855. It seems quite likely that Aytoun gave a similar lecture in Lerwick that summer and that it was in 1855 that Amelia Harris heard him speak.

[3] Amelia Harris slightly exaggerated her mother's age in this letter. Grace Dow was born on 20 July 1782 (Scott 1915-25: 5.256) and baptised on 24 July (General Register House. OPR 335/1 Blairgowrie). If she had been alive in November 1859, she would have been 77 and in her 78th year.

[4] These numbers remain the same in this edition.

[5] This tallies with Scott (1915-25: 5.397) which gives David Harris's year of birth as 1774.

the song.[6] My father had never heard the fragment of
the ballad until I repeated it to him recently.

    I have sent the M.S. by the same post as this – w^h
there is no occasion for returning – and again hoping I
have not given you unnecessary trouble, believe me
Sir

Yours most respectfully

Amelia Harris

Aytoun was appreciative of the gift and wrote of it in the
following terms in a letter of 18 November sent from 16 Great Stuart
Street, Edinburgh, and addressed to Mrs (Miss) Harris, Newburgh,
Fife. The letter is known only from an extract made by Jane Harris
which starts abruptly in mid-sentence.

> Your collection of old ballads, which, with the history
> of their being taken down, are of very great value.
> They not only give instances of variations, such as I
> have always maintained to be strong proofs of the
> antiquity of the old Ballads, but they effectually, I
> think, dispose of the theory lately started, that several
> of them, Sir Patrick Spens among the number, were
> recent forgeries. One or two of them are quite new to
> me, and seem to have escaped the diligence of former
> collectors.[7]

He also wrote at greater length about the manuscript on 12
December to Norval Clyne, an advocate in Aberdeen who shared his
interest in ballads. His letter includes the following passage.

> Since I issued the second edition of my Collection of
> the Ballads, I have received from a lady residing at
> Newburgh a most interesting M.S. being copies of
> ballads taken down by her from her mother's recitat-
> ion, with a still older pedigree. Among these is a
> version of *Sir Patrick Spens*, which differs in some
> respects from any I have yet seen. The following are
> the most important variations.

---

[6] See **19** "Andrew Cowper" / "Andrew Coupar".

[7] MS B f. 38^v. The quotation of this passage enclosed with Jane Harris's
letter to David Masson (*Harris Letters* no. 1; see below) has the reading
"others" instead of "the number".

He's gane up to the tap-mast,
  To the tap-mast so hie;
He luikit around on ilka side,
  But dry land he couldna see.

———————

He luikit on his youngest son,
  And the tear blinded his e'e, –
'I wish you had been in your mither's bouir,
  But there you'll never be!

———————

'Pray for yoursels, my merry young men,
  Pray for yoursels and me,
"For the first land in that we will land,
  Will be in the bottom ~~of~~ o' the sea!"

———————

Then up she rose, the mermaiden,
  Wi' the kaim and glass in her hand –
"Here's a health to you, my merry young
  For ye never will see dry land!"   [men

———————

O laith, laith were our gude Scots lords
  To weit their laigh-heel'd shoon,
But lang, lang or the play was play'd,
  Their yellow locks soom'd aboon.

———————

It's och, och ower to Aberdour,
  It's fifty fathom deep,
And there lie a' our gude Scots lords
  Wi' Sir Patrick at their feet.

———————

> There was Saturday, and Sabbath day,
>   And Monanday at morn,
> That Silken sheets and feather beds
>   Cam' floating to Kinghorn. &c.

Is not this very fine in its roughness? Among her Collection are two stanzas of *Brown Adam*, called by her *Brown Edom*, which must be the genuine ones, those given by Sir Walter being supposititious.

> His stithy was o' the beaten gowd,
>   His hammer o' the pith,
> And the cords were o' the gude green silk
>   He blew his bellows with.

> It fell out ance, upon a nicht,
>   Brown Edom he thought lang,
> That he wad go to see his love
>   By the lee licht o' the mune.

I cannot expect that my second edition will go off nearly so rapidly as the first, but when the time comes for a third issue, I shall certainly prepare an Appendix, containing these, and some other recent discoveries which have reached me.[8]

Since Clyne had just been engaging in a controversy that centred on *Sir Patrick Spens* the information on this ballad was of special interest to him. Robert Chambers (1859) had revived a suggestion made earlier by David Laing that Elizabeth Halket, Lady Wardlaw (1677-1727), had written, besides her acknowledged ballad-like poem, "Hardyknute", a whole set of the anonymous ballads, including *Sir Patrick Spens* with which his discussion opens.

Clyne evidently received Aytoun's letter too late to incorporate anything from it in his refutation published in 1859 entitled *The*

---

[8] This extract is quoted from a copy made by Clyne (*Harris Letters* no. 3), which was enclosed with his letter to Child of 3 May 1873 (*Harris Letters* no. 7). Clyne copied another excerpt which contains overlapping material (*Harris Letters* no. 3) and this was enclosed with his letter to John Stuart (see below). The copy sent to Stuart has "recoveries" instead of "recent discoveries" in the last sentence quoted.

Romantic Scottish Ballads and the Lady Wardlaw Heresy, but he did include three verses of *Sir Patrick Spens* from the letter in a footnote in his *Ballads from Scottish History* (Clyne 1863: 213). When James Hutton Watkins entered the fray with another refutation of Chambers's position, he published the entire section of Aytoun's letter to Clyne that deals with *Sir Patrick Spens* (1868: 465-6), but no further Harris material reached print at this time. Aytoun did not live to prepare the revised edition of his ballads that he had projected.

However, Clyne kept the Harris ballads in mind and, when Dr John Stuart of the General Register House, Edinburgh, sent on to him a request from Child for advice and information, he included an extract from Aytoun's letter when he responded to Stuart with a number of helpful suggestions in a letter of 30 September 1872 (*Harris Letters* no. 4). This was sent from 11 Union Buildings, Aberdeen, and says, in part:

> Were Mr. Child to spend a Summer in Britain his project might be greatly facilitated. Meantime the best suggestion I can offer is, that he should send to *Notes & Queries* a letter explaining it and requesting information as to the whereabouts of the desired materials. We could see to get his communication copied into various newspapers, and I trust with a substantial result ... The enclosed Excerpt from a letter sent me by Aytoun in 1859 will interest Mr. Child. I suppose the M.S. ballads he mentions may be got at without much difficulty, unless the Blackwoods have an interest in them, which I hardly think, since they appear to have made no use of them. The 3^{d} Edition Aytoun contemplated he unfortunately did not live to prepare. The two Editions issued by the Blackwoods after his death seem to be mere reprints of the 2^{d}.

Clyne's letter was forwarded to Child by Stuart on 8 October (*Harris Letters* no. 5), and Child took up the suggestion of putting a notice in *Notes and Queries.* His piece, headed "Old Ballads. Prof. Child's Appeal.", appeared on 4 January 1873 and includes the following passage (ser. 4, vol. 11, p. 12):

But it is not only original copies of printed ballads that I am desirous to obtain. There are doubtless *unprinted* manuscripts of ballads in existence. A "most interesting" one was sent Aytoun by a lady in Fifeshire some thirteen years ago, and would have been used by him had he lived to make a third edition of his collection.

Clyne involved himself very actively in furthering Child's search and reported his activities to Child in a letter dated 21 January (*Child MSS* vol. 26, nos 1726-7):

On the "Appeal" appearing in N & Q I did my best to "raise the country" in support of it by communicating with a number of Newspaper Editors from Inverness to Fifeshire and suggesting their copying it. ...

About the unpublished M.S.S. obtained by Aytoun I wrote to Theodore Martin his friend and biographer, who replied that he had never heard of them, and advised an enquiry of Mr John Blackwood or of Misses Aytoun – "like their brother, passionately fond of old Ballads". I preferred the latter course and wrote to Miss Aytoun (Edinburgh) explaining what was particularly wanted, and saying that if she could give any information on the subject or the address of the "lady in Newburgh," you would, I was sure, be happy to communicate with them direct. After a fortnight I have a note from Miss Aytoun, mentioning that her sister and she had none of their brothers M.S. ballads and that, on speaking to Mr. Blackwood, she found he knew nothing of those wanted, and regretting her inability "to assist Prof. Child in his new work". A possible explanation of the mystery has been suggested to me by a friend well acquainted with the family. Aytoun's second wife married again, and his relatives are not on friendly terms with her. *She* may be in possession of the treasure we seek for, and I expect to get her exact address very shortly for the purpose of asking her the question. Should this fail I will have enquiries made in Newburgh itself.

Clyne drew a blank also with Aytoun's widow (*Harris Letters* no. 7: Clyne to Child, 3 May 1873), and, as he had promised, he had enquiries made in Newburgh. His contact there was a banker and historian, Alexander Laing, who made considerable efforts but met with no success.[9]

Meanwhile, on the very same day that Clyne wrote to Child about his failure to trace the manuscript that had been sent by Amelia Harris to Aytoun in 1859, Jane Harris was writing about a newly prepared manuscript to Professor David Masson, who had succeeded Aytoun as Professor of Rhetoric at the University of Edinburgh. She makes no mention of Child's appeal but, considering the newspaper coverage it had been given, it seems not unlikely that it was this that stimulated the writing of the letter, though not the preparation of the manuscript which had gone on for some time. Her letter, headed January 21st –73 and sent from Laurel Bank, Lasswade, Edinburgh, to Professor Masson, University, Edinburgh, runs (*Harris Letters* no. 6):

> Sir,
>   Possessing a valuable collection of old unpublished Ballads, and Ballad Airs and being anxious to dispose of them, I have found great difficulty in ascertaining their actual value, or in finding the proper channels for bringing them fully before the collectors of such – A Friend the other day suggested that you might not be unwilling to advise me, but having no personal introduction unfortunately, and fully aware of the numerous claims on y^r valuable time, with much hesitancy I venture to request y^r kindness in giving me an idea of their pecuniary value, or the better mode of bringing them under the notice of parties interested. My Sister shewed the Ballads to the late Professor Ayton, in 1859, she received a very flattering reply as to their worth, a copy of his note I now enclose. The Ballad Airs, I arranged in a simple way for the Piano last winter, and in addition have added a subsequent

---

[9] *Child MSS* vol. 1, pp. 82-3: Clyne to Child, February 1873; *Harris Letters* no. 7: Clyne to Child, 3 May 1873; *Child MSS* vol. 27, nos 2043-4: Clyne to Child, 17 June 1873; *Ballad MS of Alexander Laing of Newburgh on Tay* (Houghton Library MS 25241.43*), nos 1, 2 and 3: Laing to Clyne, 11 February 1873; Laing to Clyne, 18 August 1873; Laing to Child, 12 June 1873.

stock, gathered from old domestics and peasantry in my late Father's parish, w^h also form *their* link of history, in the Ballad singing of that period – we consider the Airs alone of importance, their ballads being still widely in type, while unaware that the music has ever been committed to notation:– From circumstances, I consider that both Ballads, w^h are mostly varieties of those already published, and Airs, have been preserved in great purity, being sung by us, just precisely as done in my Great-Father's Manse at Tibbermore 150 years ago. Should you kindly accede to my request, I would be glad, either to wait upon you, or transmit my M.S.S. by post, as might best be agreeable to you. And with many apologies for the liberty I have taken in writing you,

Believe me,

Most Respectfully,

Jane Harris.

This letter was sent on to Child who, when writing from Harvard to William Macmath in Edinburgh on 9 May about his general disappointment with the results of the appeal, mentions that: "I have however, hopes that Mr Norval Clyne of Aberdeen may be able to recover some pieces once offered Aytoun, & that a Miss Harris, who writes Prof Masson about certain new pieces collected by herself, may let me have them." (Reppert 1953: no. 23) Clyne, in a letter to Child of 3 May, had already suggested that there might be a connection with the "Newburgh lady" that they were in search of, saying, "Could the *Miss Harris* you mention by any possibility be that 'lady' we want?" By August, the connection had been established and Clyne sent Child an account of his meeting with the Harris sisters (*Harris Letters* no. 8).

11 Union Buildings.

Aberdeen, 27 Aug. 1873

My Dear Sir

Miss Harris and Miss Jane Harris and their M.S. Ballads honoured me with their company at Tea last night. Although Miss Jane appears to be the correspondent her elder sister (Amelia) is the writer of the MS ~~Ballads~~ and the repository of the Ballads, of

xxv

which she has recorded the descent in an unusually
satisfactory way. Their father lived to be the oldest
Parish Minister in Scotland and *his* father and
Grandfather were Ministers before him. Miss Harris'
mother, who chiefly taught her the words (and music
also) was born in 1782 and was herself taught them by
an aged nurse. So old a hand is Miss H. as a
collector that she wrote down, when a girl, one or
two ballads which were sent to Peter Buchan, and they
appear in his Collection (without acknowledgement I
think) but with such variations as may, as Miss H.
admits, represent more accurate versions otherwise
recovered by him. Several of her Ballads are new to
me as they were to Aytoun and the versions of others
are remarkably different from the printed copies.
She says that in order to keep her own memory – a
very good one – clear from outside influences since
her mother's death, she has abstained from reading
published collections.

The enclosed list [see Appendix A] was sent me
by Miss H. before she came to Aberdeen and will in
the meantime give you an idea of the Contents of the
M.S. Several of the pieces are only fragments.

The set she sent to Aytoun was not so complete.
Believing no doubt that he was left to make use of
them (and Miss H. says she wrote in such a way as
likely to lead him to believe so) he did not return the
M.S. and it is now lost, or destroyed since his death.

All I can gather about her pecuniary views is that
she *does* put a money value on the M.S. and that she
has been offered something by somebody, who said
that if she lent ~~them~~ it to any other body he would
withdraw his offer. She is personally an exceedingly
pleasant lady, with means apparently sufficient to
enable her to live comfortably and ramble here and
there, as she and her sister have just been doing. She
leaves Aberdeen tomorrow and is to call again before
doing so. I will see whether she has any suggestion to
make about the perusal of her papers by yourself or
some one on your behalf – say Dr David Laing. She
must see that this is necessary before any sum can be
offered for the right to print.

In case, as is not unlikely, you may have to communicate with her directly, – as I daresay she would prefer – I give her home address –

Miss Harris
Laurel Bank
Lasswade
Edinburgh

I ought to mention that she lived for 2 years in Newburgh. I have just sent Mr. Laing a note about her. The ladies told me that the reason why they were not acquainted except by name with Mr. Laing and the old ladies he speaks of in his letters, was, that Newburgh society was divided into Whigs and Tories whose political principles ruled it in every thing, and that the Harris family were Whigs while the other people were of the opposite faction!

30 August
Since writing, I have seen Miss H. but only on the street, and all she told me was that she would not be at home until beginning of October. There can hardly, therefore, be further communication with her till then. I think your advisable course is not to be in a hurry writing to her, in case the apparent anxiety to secure her ballads may give her an exaggerated notion of their value pecuniarily. It strikes me she will, after a little, return to the subject herself. When you do write to her, perhaps you should ask her to shew the M.S. to Dr Laing with the view of his suggesting an offer. I wish she were as confiding as in 1859!

Yours ever faithfully
Norval Clyne

By this time Child was in Britain. He was in Edinburgh on 8 August and in Glasgow on 23 August, and afterwards spent some time in London where he was a guest at the home of the mediaevalist, F. J. Furnivall, at 3 St George's Square, Primrose Hill.[10]

---

[10] Edinburgh – Macmath statement and Macmath to Child, Reppert 1953: nos 25-6; Glasgow – Child to Macmath, Reppert 1953: no. 28; London – Child-Macmath correspondence, Reppert 1953: nos 29-31.

Writing to Macmath from there on 9 September, Child notes the successes that had attended his visit to Britain.

> You will be glad to learn that I have the loan of Motherwell's MS., from Glasgow, an important book of nearly 700 pp. This I am having copied. I have also found the missing woman who lent her ballads to Aytoun. So the Summer has not been a vain one. (Reppert 1953: no. 31)

He was to leave England on 18 September (Child to Macmath, 23 August; Reppert 1953: no. 28) and was evidently keen to have the manuscript in his possession before that date. The close of the transaction is recorded in a letter sent to Child at Furnivall's home by Amelia Harris from 21 Dick Place, Edinburgh, on 15 September.[11]

> Dear Sir,
> This morning I received a Telegram from Mr. Furnival informing me that he had forwarded a cheque for £15 Price of the M.S.S. which I shall not fail to acknowlege on receipt. I shall send on the M.S. of Ballads, registered, by Book post this afternoon, and the M.S. Music tomorrow, as my sister has to add the Bass, to the last addition of the more modern airs. I have not lost hopes of recovering a few more verses, having several friends in rural districts to whom I have appealed. I recollect our family Doctor, at Newburgh a very intelligent, and enthusiastic man, showed us a M.S. copy of "Robin he's gaen to the Wude", different from that in my collection[12] but a very fine complete variation – It may be of use to you to correspond with him, he is now at the head of the Medical Mission Training department at Glasgow – I much regret being unable to give his distinct address.
> My mother often remarked that she had only a tithe of old Jannie Scott's ballads – some of them were too coarse for singing – she did not sing them to us, if she kept them in mind, and what we saw in the hawkers baskets we did not trouble to commit to

---

[11] *Harris Letters* no. 9. 21 Dick Place was the home of Miss Marjory Seymour (*Edinburgh Post Office Directory* 1873).

[12] See **21** "Robin" / "Robin He's gane to the wude".

memory. If you require any reference, I will be happy
to assist to the best of my ability.
Yours very truly
Amelia Harris.

P.S I see I have omitted to give the Dr' name
John Lyall. M.D.
A.H.

Child had noted in his correspondence with Macmath that "from
the 16th on it will be safer to address me in America" (Reppert
1953: no. 28) so the Harris material was being sent to him at the last
possible moment, Amelia's portion of it on the 15th and Jane's on
the 16th. On 9 January 1874, Child, writing to Macmath from
Harvard, noted that "Miss Harris's" manuscript was among his
acquisitions (Reppert 1953: no. 52) and two records at the beginning
of the manuscript itself dated 28 March 1874 state that it was
"bought with the income from the subscription fund begun in 1858"
and that it cost £15, plus 6 shillings for the binding. The payment in
sterling for the binding implies that the binding was done in Britain
and there are several indications that Furnivall took responsibility for
the manuscript for a time.

This Harris MS (MS B in this edition) is Houghton Library MS
25241.17*. It is bound in 3/4 maroon morocco and marbled boards.
The spine has largely perished but some lettering is still legible. The
manuscript is in two parts. Furnivall wrote "Part I. Ballads" on f. 1r,
which also carries in Amelia Harris's hand the heading: "Amelia
Harris' Collection of Traditional Antient Ballads, and Fragments,
also including songs of more recent date". Furnivall also wrote "Part
II. Music" on f. 38r which has on the verso the statement in Jane
Harris's hand: "The Ballad Airs now set have one history with the
Ballads first written down and forwarded to the late Professor
Aytoun in 1859: being orally, and directly traced from my Great
Father's (Rev P. Duncan, Tibbermore) manse, from 1745, and are
precisely set, as sung by my mother to her, then, youthful family.
Jane Harris, March, 1872. Laurel Bank."

The collation is as follows: PART I [1^4 2^6 3^4 4^8 5^4 6^8 (-6_8) 7^4] = 37
leaves (29.8 x 23.6 cm). Signatures [1-6] are on wove paper, no
watermark. Signature [7] is on laid paper, watermarked: A.
ANNANDALE & SONS. A leaf of laid paper (22.8 x 17.5 cm.) is
inserted after folio 3. PART II. 8 leaves of music, in wrapper, foliated
(including wrapper) 38-47 (45-47 blank). Wove paper; the wrapper is
on a thinner stock, resembling the paper of signatures [1-6] in Part I.

The cancellation of leaf [6₈], and the insertion of a new gathering on another paper (signature [7]) suggest afterthoughts.

The leaf inserted after folio 3 contains a numbered list of the contents of Part I in ink in a hand which is identified in a note made by George Lyman Kittredge as Dr Furnivall's. The texts in Part I were numbered by Amelia at or near the title. She apparently initially wrote the first twenty-one songs without numbering since these numbers are in pencil, unlike the texts, which are in ink throughout. From 22 onwards the numbers appear in ink (except for a pencilled 23) and seem to have been written along with the texts. The numbers run correctly in sequence up to 40 but there is then a jump to 42 at the point where the change occurs from wove to laid paper making it seem probable that the misnumbering is associated with the change and suggesting the possibility that the cancelled leaf, [6₈], had on it an item numbered 41. However, the items numbered 42-51 are actually 41-50 in the collection as we have it and Furnivall indicated this by correcting the numbers in his list. In this edition, the correct number in the sequence is given for these ten songs followed by Amelia Harris's number in square brackets. In Part II, Jane Harris numbered the music items clearly in the margin but omitted 25 so that the items 25-7 are 26-8 in her numbering. She failed to number the 28th item and so 29 and 30 are correctly numbered. However, the number 30 is repeated for the 31st item. The correct sequence numbers are given here but Jane Harris's different numbers for four of the songs are included in square brackets.

The earlier Harris MS (MS A in this edition) was never located by Child and its history after Aytoun's death is obscure. However, it can be said that the name of one owner, "Capt. Forbes, R.N., Seabank" appears on the fly-leaf and that the bound manuscript was discovered by Mr Hilary Corke among other Forbes books in an Edinburgh bookshop-depository that dated back before 1939 and had not been disturbed between that time and the date of finding in 1955.[13] Having observed Amelia Harris's reference in her letter to Aytoun to the writing down of the airs, Corke made an intensive search for the airs in the depository and was satisfied that they were not there.

Corke, who was a lecturer in Mediaeval English Literature at the University of Edinburgh, fully appreciated the value of what he had found and wrote to Harvard on 29 November 1955 describing the contents of his manuscript and asking for information about the Harris MS listed by Child as being in Harvard College Library. His

---

[13] Letter from Hilary Corke to Emily Lyle dated 12 April 1975.

correspondence with W. H. Bond, Curator of the Houghton Library, was made available to me when I was working through Child's papers in 1974-5 and this allowed me to make the first mention in print of Corke's important discovery (Lyle 1977: 127).

The manuscript, which appears to have been bound under Aytoun's direction, is in very good condition. It has a maroon cover with the wording "M.S. OLD SCOTTISH BALLADS" on its spine, and has marbled endpapers with Hilary Corke's bookplate inside the front cover. The material sent by Amelia Harris is on 26 folios of unwatermarked paper (22.6 x 18.6 cm). The folios were numbered by Corke in pencil on either side as pages 1-52 and his page numbering has been used in this edition. All but two (nos **14** and **17**) of the twenty-nine songs were numbered by Amelia Harris beside the title; through an error in binding the folio containing **21** "Robin" occurs at the end (pp. 51-2). The folios containing the texts are interleaved with paper watermarked: J WHATMAN 1859, which had been blank until the addition of pencilled notes by Corke on the variations of five ballads from the versions in Child.[1]   The letter to Aytoun has been bound in before the ballads. It is accompanied by its envelope which has postal marks made in Newburgh and Edinburgh with the date 1859. The binding is so tight that it is not possible to open the book flat and this has meant that photographic reproduction of any part of MS A has not been feasible.

Emily Lyle

---

[1] The ballads are nos **1, 6, 12, 14** and **18**.

The Harris family and their contacts

David and Grace Harris had seven children of whom Amelia (b. 7 April 1815) was the second and Jane (b. 18 January 1823) the sixth.[15] The others were Mary (1813-1849), George (1818-1860), Grace (1819-1842), Elizabeth (1821-1840) and William (b. 1825) (Scott 1915-25: 5.397). The children were brought up in the village of Fearn in the hills of Angus, of which their father was the minister.[16]

When Amelia wrote to Aytoun from Newburgh in November 1859, she was 44 years old and Jane was 36. Their three sisters had died by this date and William had emigrated to Canada.[17] George (who succeeded their father as minister of Fearn in 1854) died in the following year.[18]

On 21 January 1873, when Jane wrote to Masson, she had just turned 49 and Amelia was 55. At this time the sisters were living at Lasswade, a village some eight miles east of Edinburgh, but shortly afterwards they established themselves at Canaan Villa, 2 Canaan Lane, in Morningside, Edinburgh,[19] and remained there until death. Amelia died on 16 January 1891, aged 75, leaving the bulk of her

---

[15] Amelia, 7 April 1815 – 16 January 1891. Jane, 18 January 1823 – 2 September 1897. Birth dates are from Scott (1915-25: 5.397), the death dates from records of death held in Register House.

[16] It was David Harris who provided the account of Fearn parish for the *New Statistical Account of Scotland*. He remarked upon its geographic isolation, noting that it lay "a great distance from any great market-town" (1845: 315), and also its social isolation, Fearn having "no tavern, no news-room, no lodge, no clubs, and no special association, civil, social, or religious, which we can call our own". He also comments upon the bad state of the local roads, the fact that "no line of turnpike passes through the parish, and the same may be said with regard to stage-coaches" (p. 319) and that the inhabitants of Fearn had "the two highest pinnacles in the country round" to climb before reaching Brechin, which lay only six miles from the parish.

[17] Contact was apparently lost with the youngest brother, William. In the sisters' joint will, made 4 October 1890 (SCO 70/4/250, 34-6), he is bequeathed a memento "if alive". This will gives his last known location as Toronto (SCO 70/4/250, 35).

[18] Scott 1915-25: 5.397. According to an entry in *Angus or Forfarshire, the Land and People* (Warden 1880-5: 3.267), George had "studied medicine, and being kind-hearted and of an amiable disposition, he was ever ready to attend to the temporal ailments, and administer spiritual comforts, to the poor in his own and the neighbouring parishes, and was beloved in the district".

[19] They are listed at this address in the *Edinburgh and Leith Post Office Directory* for 1874-5. The site is now a car park.

estate to Jane.[20] In 1897, Jane was removed to Longmore Hospital in Salisbury Place, Newington, and died there on 2 September, aged 74.[21] Both sisters were buried in Warriston Cemetery.[22]

In Jane's will there is no mention of family, although legacies were left to one Mrs Janet Burnside and her three daughters. Jane directed that the remainder of any free funds should be made over to the Edinburgh Fund for the Relief of Indigent Gentlewomen of Scotland.[23]

No family papers have been located and we are dependent for most of our information on the correspondence and comments connected with the collection of songs. Fortunately, both sisters made explicit statements about their family background and about how they understood that the ballads and songs heard from their mother had come down to her. In addition to the passages already quoted in this introduction, there is the following statement by Amelia at the beginning of MS B:

> Nearly the whole of the following Ballads and fragments, were obtained more than forty years ago from my Mother, the late Mrs Harris of Fearn; and so far as I am concerned are traditionally pure, having been committed to memory before I saw any collection in print. Mrs Harris was daughter of the Revd William Dow, Minister of the Parish of Blairgowrie Perthshire, and was born in 1782, was left an orphan in childhood, and was placed under the care of an old nurse, whose store of antient Ballad lore was inexhaustible; and who never wearied chaunting them to her youthful listener, who picked up a mere tithe of Jannie Scott's old songs, before she was ten years of age, about which time she changed her place of residence, so that they can thus be traced by direct transmission about 150 years back.[24]

---

[20] General Register House. List of Inventory. SCO 70/1/292/267.

[21] General Register House. OPR death records, ref. 685/5 – 893.

[22] Information from Jane Harris's will (SCO 70/4/301, 673-4). The plot is identified as M 303. At present, nothing marks the plot, although in 1998 a tombstone base without names was present. The upright portion may survive among the toppled stones in the vicinity. Restoration in this neglected part of the cemetery is scheduled.

[23] General Register House. Will of Jane Harris. SCO 70/4/301, 671.

[24] Introduction to MS B, f. I[v].

From this and other statements of Amelia's (pp. xviii, xxvi and xxix) and references by Jane to Patrick Duncan's manse at Tibbermore (pp. xxv and xxix) we are given a fairly clear, if restricted, view of the relevant family history. Grace Dow's father, the Reverend William Dow, died on 13 May 1786 when she was three and her mother, Mary Dow (née Duncan) died on 21 May 1790 when she was seven (Scott 1915-25: 5.256). Grace was cared for up to the age of about ten by an old woman called Jannie Scott who had been a nurse in her mother's childhood home, the manse of her grandfather, the Reverend Patrick Duncan, who was minister at Tibbermore from 1741 until his death in 1761 (Scott 1915-25: 4.255). Jane conveys the idea that it was understood that Jannie Scott had sung to the children at the manse a generation before Grace Dow's time, and she says (p. xxix) that the songs can be traced from 1745, which was the year of birth of her grandmother, Mary Duncan (Scott 1915-25: 4.255).

Although Amelia concentrates mainly on family connections in her statement in MS B, she adds: "A few versions and fragments were gathered by myself among the peasantry and are of interest, as marking a tradition." Jane, too, speaks of some items in MS B as having been "gathered from old domestics and peasantry in my late Father's parish" (*Harris Letters* no. 6; see p. xxv above).

The informants named in MS B to whom these statements might apply are:

> Adam Duncan, Brechin **(41)**
> Mrs Isdale, Dron **(26)**
> Mrs McKenzie, Borry **(39)**
> Mrs Molison, Dunlappin **(35, 36)**
> Miss Seymour, Lethnot **(32)**[25]
> Anne Skain **(56)**
> Wilson, a servant, Fearn Manse **(34)**

The type of material gathered from those sources, in terms of ballad study, is less remarkable than that in Mrs Harris's corpus. There are only two full ballad versions, both from Mrs Molison – "Lord Revel" and "Prince Robert" – and fragments of *Rob Roy* and *Lamkin* from Mrs Isdale and Miss Seymour. The other items are songs: "Mosey, Mare" **(34)**; "A Wee Bittie East There Leeved a

---

[25] The possibility of a connection with the Miss Marjory Seymour from whose home in Edinburgh Amelia wrote to Child (see p. xxviii above) should be noted.

Man" (**39**) which is humorous; the opening of "Hie Marshall" (**56**), a song which relates to an actual incident – Lord Elgin's affair with Rose Anderson of Perth; and the sentimental "Hark Niebour Here" (**41**). Only two of the songs (**41** and **56**) have tunes.

At the end of Jane Harris's song lists [2] and [3] (the first words and the other to music), are a number of items that are absent from the collection. These are:

1 Nae Dominie/dominie for me ([2], no. 41; [3], no. 34)
2 Whaur are ye gaen ([2], no. 42)
3 Sailor Laddie ([2], no. 43; [3], no. 35)
4 The Banks o'/of the Nile ([2], no. 44; [3], no. 36)
5 The Duke o' Gordon had &c ([3], deleted entry no. 32)
6 The bonnie Sailor Laddie ([3], no. 32)
7 A lang cravat ([3], no. 33)
8 Feckless Fanny ([3], no. 37)

Item 1 is "Nae Dominie's for me, laddie" (Johnson no. 489; GD 872), item 4 is "The Banks of the Nile" (GD 99) and item 5 is "The Duke of Gordon's Daughter" (Child 237; also GD 1099), the opening line of which is "The Duke o' Gordon had three bonnie daughters" or something similar. Item 2 could be "The Soldier Lad" (GD 791) which can have the title "Where Are Ye Gaun" and normally includes a verse which begins with lines like "Where are ye gaun, my bonnie lass, / Where are ye gaun my honey". Similar material occurs in "Seventeen Come Sunday" and "My Rolling Eye" that can be regarded either as versions of the same song or as related songs. The rather general titles of items 2 and 6 have not been pinned down to particular songs, but cf. "The Sailor Laddie" (GD 55). Item 7 "A lang cravat" and item 8 "Feckless Fanny" have not been identified. Another possible extra song is "The sma' Caiterin", no. 44 in list [1]. It is suggested that this may be a reference to the "Rob Roy" fragment in the collection (**26**); if it is not, it has not been identified.

Kaye McAlpine

The music

The tunes and basses provided by Miss Jane Harris to thirty of the fifty-nine song texts (with one tune untexted) present numerous challenges to the editor. From the correspondence accompanying the MS and from evidence of the songs themselves, it is apparent that Jane wrote down the tunes, not directly from the singing of her sister, but from her own memory of the songs, as handed down by her mother to both sisters.[26] Nothing is known of her musical background, but from the manuscript it is clear that her knowledge of music notation was sketchy, particularly in regard to rhythm and harmony. A cursory reading of virtually any of the tunes as notated shows discrepancies between the time signature provided and the number of beats in a measure and raises questions about the length of note values chosen in many instances (see no. **2**, "Sir Colin" , for a clear example). Errors in pitch are much harder to detect, since making changes in pitch is a hallmark of oral tradition, and discrepancies between the pitch content of tunes in the Harris MS and any other version of the same tune in most cases could be attributed equally well to the vagaries of oral tradition as to inaccurate notation. Exceptions to this occur in nos **19** and **41**, where changes in pitch have been suggested in order to bring musical sense to the tune. The basses provided are a different case altogether. Jane Harris wrote in her letter to Professor David Masson describing the collection, "The Ballad Airs, *I arranged in a simple way for the Piano last winter ...*"[27] [editor's italics], indicating that the basses were added in order to make them into pieces suitable for the piano – or at least for piano accompaniment. There is no mention in the correspondence of the use of piano accompaniment by either her mother or sister. Indeed, from another letter, it is clear that at least in some cases, the basses were added after the writing down of the tune itself.[28] The basses are therefore, in the opinion of this editor, of interest only as the mid- to late-nineteenth-century practice of at least some performers (perhaps

---

[26] One sign that Jane worked from her own memory rather than from the singing of her sister is that in the first verse underlay that is normally included (sometimes it is a later verse), there are often minor variants of words and word-order, differing from either of her sister's text-versions in MS A and MS B. We also know that the tune MS was sent in at least one day later than were the texts (see letter of 15 September 1873 from Amelia Harris to Child) in order for Jane to complete her musical work.

[27] Letter of 21 January 1873; see above, pp. xxiv-v.

[28] Letter of 15 September 1873 from Amelia Harris to Child; see above, pp. xxviii-ix.

in response to a perceived necessity to "dress up the tunes" for scholarly or artistic scrutiny), but of no particular value in the longer tradition of the ballad tunes as handed down from the eighteenth century. The basses are accordingly only represented here in facsimile. They are often incompetent by the standards of mid-nineteenth-century harmonic practice (see especially nos **6**, **10**, **19**, **30**, **40** and **52**), and in ten tunes whole sections of the bass accompaniment are omitted (see, for example, nos **4** and **10**; all but one measure of the bass for no. **42** is missing). Most often the basses are single-line, but in twelve tunes there are octave doublings and/or simple harmonies on occasional notes. Strikingly, these chords are often found in tunes for which the bass is incomplete. Occasionally there is a bass-line that is rather felicitous by modern standards (see, for example, no. **11**, bars 7-8). The whole harmonisation of tune no. **57** is better than average.

The problem of editing these tunes, then, is to guess the intention of the transcriber through the veil of her semi-competent notation. When she writes a dotted minim followed by a quaver instead of the more logical dotted-crotchet/quaver combination, for instance, is this simply a mistake, or her way of attempting to show that the first note was actually held longer? (See no. **3**, bar 1.) She employs a variety of additional markings that could also indicate lengthening. These include a straight line over a note (see facsimiles for nos **7**, **12**, **18**, **29**, **40**, **42**, **52**, **55**); a straight line with a dot underneath (no. **2**); a fermata (nos **2**, **6**, **11**, **16**, **30**, **40**, **55**, **58**); an inverted fermata under the note (no. **5**); a v-shaped fermata (no. **16**); and a v-shaped fermata without the dot (nos **4**, **56**). Perhaps these various markings were attempts to indicate a flexible approach to rhythm which is rather typical of much of Scottish ballad tradition and notoriously difficult to transcribe into any conventional notation system.

Because of the extensive rhythmic problems, drastic editing was at times necessary to make the tunes minimally intelligible, and decisions were made based on this editor's knowledge of the Scottish tune tradition.

Without such editing it is probable that even a musically literate ballad scholar might find the task of making sense of the tunes with their texts unnecessarily daunting.[29] Other choices could also be valid, which is why a facsimile of the original is provided for comparison.

---

[29] The most extensive rhythmic changes are found in nos **10**, **11**, **12**, **13**, **18**, **29**, **52**, **53**, **54**.

The two other publications that have presented the tunes of this MS are Child (1882-98) and Bronson (1959-72). In addition, Bronson's article "Professor Child's Ballad Tunes", *California Folklore Quarterly* 1 (1942-43), presents the Harris MS on pp. 192-4, with Bronson's own thoughts on the validity of the Jane Harris notation. Except for omitting any mention of the bass lines and misrepresenting the number of tunes in the MS (Bronson states that "the MS contains at present twenty-three tunes" when there are actually thirty-one tunes, although only twenty-three are published in Child as being from the Harris MS), the article is a factual account of the differences between what Child published (which was actually edited by Child's assistant, Professor W. R. Spalding, of the Harvard Department of Music) and what is in the MS. When there are discrepancies, Bronson gives his own interpretation, which is usually close to the versions he eventually published in *Traditional Tunes*. His main aim seems to be to preserve the rhythmic relationships in the MS, and by means of re-barring and a liberal use of changing and irregular meters (such as 5/4) he can sometimes preserve Jane Harris's idiosyncratic note values, which he feels "give valuable clues as to the way in which the songs were actually sung which might have been obliterated by a more experienced musician" (Bronson 1942-43: 193). This could well be true, though many of the rhythmic mistakes are those typically made by students not yet well versed in notation.[30]

General musical characteristics

Most of the tunes are the traditional four-phrase ballad tunes, with the exception of four five-phrase tunes and one of six phrases (no. **17**). There is also one tune with two strains (eight phrases), "The Battle of La Hogue" no. **52**. The most common overall form is ABCD (fourteen tunes), followed by ABAC or ABA'C (six tunes), AA'BC (two tunes), and AA'BA", ABA'B, and ABB'C (one tune each). The tunes have the usual alternation of four and three accents per phrase, or four plus four. Only three tunes use the double-length line of 7, 7, 7, 7 (nos **11** and **18**, with no. **52** having double that number).

The ranges of the tunes are between an octave (seven tunes) and a 12th (two tunes), with ranges of a 9th (seven tunes), a 10th (twelve tunes) and an 11th (three tunes). Large leaps are relatively common,

---

[30] Oral communication from Professor Robert Hurwitz, University of Oregon, specialist in theory pedagogy.

as in much of Scottish folksong. Leaps of an octave or a sixth downward predominate (see nos **2**, **3**, **4**, **6**, **10**, **19**, **30**, **31**, **40**, **53**, **55** and **57**), often in the third phrase; while upward leaps of an octave are slightly less common (see nos **6**, **7**, **12**, **14**, **16**, **19**, **25**, **30**, **40, 42**, **52** and **57**).

Scales used are predominantly 7-note (heptatonic), with fourteen tunes, followed by various forms of hexatonic scales: those without the 4th degree (eight tunes), without the 7th (three tunes), and without the 6th (four tunes). There are only two pentatonic tunes: no. **42** without 3rd and 7th, and no. **55** without 4th and 7th. Eight of the tunes have a flat 3rd, bringing them into a minor modality; nine have a flat 7th; one has a flat 6th. (No. **3** has the 3rd, 6th and 7th flatted; seven tunes have both the 3rd and 7th flatted.)

While the tunes as a group have many tonal patterns in common, only two of them seem so closely related to one another in melodic contour as to constitute possible variants; these are nos **41** "Hark Niebour here", and **53** "There cam a Ghost". In short, there is a remarkable variety among these thirty-one tunes. Their aesthetic quality and singability is likewise mixed. There are some exquisite tunes among the thirty-one once the notational difficulties have been ironed out (see especially nos **3**, **4**, **5**, **11**, **16**, **18** and **29**). The percentage of the Harris MS tunes which form part of the Child canon is remarkable; it would seem that Professor Child relied heavily on these MSS for the formation of a portion of his collection.

Anne Dhu McLucas

Editorial practice

Amelia Harris was responsible for all the Harris material in MS A and for all but the music section of MS B. The following remarks apply to the editing of her work in both manuscripts. She writes in a bold hand which is generally legible but there is some ambiguity about certain letters. The letter "w" can be written with two minims only and, in this form, is indistinguishable from "u". When the letter is formed like a "u" it is read as "u", except in those cases where "u" is not a possible alternative spelling when it is read as "w", as in "twa". Although the letters "i" and "e" are generally clearly written, the "i" can be undotted and written in an open form like an "e" and there is sometimes no open space in the letter "e", so that there is some ambiguity, particularly when the two letters come together. The exclamation mark is sometimes written fully but is quite often indicated by a mere tick. Quotation marks are given erratically in either the double or single form and this feature has been retained. While closing quotation marks are often outside the closing full-stop or comma, they sometimes come immediately above or before this mark. In this edition, all closing quotation marks are shown after the full-stop or comma. The breadth of the paper allows complete lines of the songs to be given without turning. The verses are generally divided by a small space. The few cases where there is some doubt about verse division are indicated in the notes. No verse numbers are given and the verse numbering here is editorial. The indenting of the songs follows Amelia Harris's practice of indenting where there are alternate rhymes. She is generally careful about this but is not totally consistent and this edition has normalised this presentation feature. The refrains are written out in full or in part as shown here. Amelia generally indicates omissions by a line or two of crosses; these omissions are shown here by lines of dots. She occasionally simply leaves gaps in incomplete lines (e.g. at 5B 16.3) and these gaps appear in the same way in the printed texts. The few words that are underlined in the manuscript are printed in italics.

The title printed at the head of the MS B text is that given by Amelia Harris except in **53-59** which are present only in Jane's music section of the manuscript. Where Jane had a different title in **1-52**, this is included in the notes. The ascriptions shown in brackets after the titles are taken from Amelia's texts in **1-52** and from the music headings in **53-59**, except that, in the case of **40** "Tod Lowrie", the words "& others" have been added from the music heading, and that at **27** "The higher that the mountain is" and **28** "Hech hiegh Durham" the ascription to David Harris is taken from Amelia's letter to Aytoun (p. xviii). All the titles written above the music are in Jane's hand. However, all the ascriptions to sources with the music are in Amelia's hand with the exception of the ascription to Anne Skain at **56** "Hie Marshall" which is in Jane's.

The music is found only in MS B. Each tune is given here in facsimile at the head of the B text while the edited printed version is shown either opposite the facsimile version at the head of the A text, where there is one, or else following it.

Emily Lyle

PART 1

SONGS APPEARING IN MS A
WITH PARALLELS FROM MS B

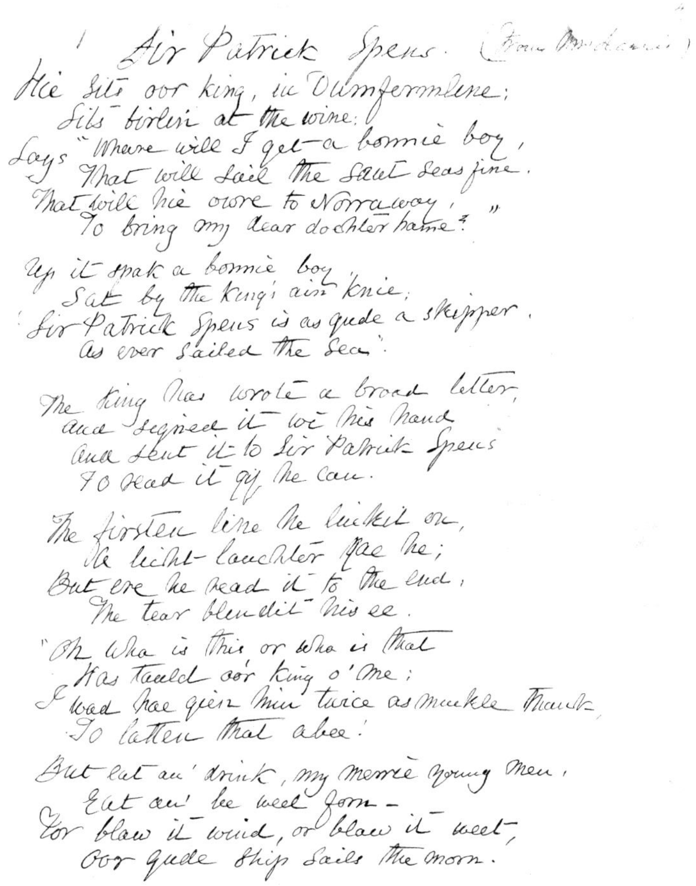

Air Patrick Spens. (from ...)

Hie sits oor king, in Dumfermline;
  Sits birlin at the wine:
Says "Whare will I get a bonnie boy,
  That will sail the saut seas fine.
That will hie owre to Norraway,
  To bring my dear dochter hame?"

Up it spak a bonnie boy,
  Sat by the king's ain knie;
Sir Patrick Spens is as gude a skipper.
  As ever sailed the sea.

The king has wrote a broad letter,
  And signed it wi his hand
  And sent it to Sir Patrick Spens
  To read it off he can.

The firsten line he lickit on,
  A licht lauchter gae he;
But ere he read it to the end,
  The tear blendit his ee.

"Oh wha is this or wha is that
  Has tauld oor king o' me;
I wad hae gien him twice as muckle thanks,
  To latten that abee.

But eat an' drink, my merrie young men,
  Eat an' be weel forn –
For blaw it wind, or blaw it weet,
  Oor gude ship sails the morn.

Fig. 3 The opening of "Sir Patrick Spens" in the hand of
Amelia Harris (MS B, f. 4[r]).

1

p. 1

Sir Patrick Spens
[Child no. 58 Sir Patrick Spens]

Hie sits our King— in Dun-ferm-line, Sits bir-lin' at the wine. Says,

whaur will I get a bon-nie boy, Will sail the saut seas— fine.

1   Hie sits our king in Dunfermline,
     Sits birl'in at the wine. –
    Says "Whaur will I get a bonnie boy
     That will sail the saut seas fine
    That will haud ower to Norawa
     And bring my dear dochter hame?"

2   Up an' spak a bonnie boy
     Wha sat by the king's ain knee
    'Sir Patrick Spens is as gude a skipper
     As ever sailed the sea –"

3   The King has wrote a broad letter
     An' sealed it wi his hand
    And sent it to Sir Patrick Spens
     To read it if he can.

4   The first an' line he luikit on
     A licht lauchter gae he
    But ere he read it to the end
     The tear blinded his ee'.

1

Sir Patrick Spens   (From Mrs Harris)
[Child no. 58 Sir Patrick Spens]

f. 39ʳ
no. 3

1   Hie sits oor king, in Dumfermline;   f. 4ʳ
       Sits birlin at the wine: no. 1
    Says "Whare will I get a bonnie boy,
       That will sail the saut seas fine.
    That will hie owre to Norraway,
       To bring my dear dochter hame?"

2   Up it spak a bonnie boy,
       Sat by the king's ain knie;
    'Sir Patrick Spens is as gude a skipper,
       As ever sailed the sea."

3   The king has wrote a broad letter,
       And signed it wi his hand
    And sent it to Sir Patrick Spens
       To read it gif he can.

4   The firsten line he luikit on,
       A licht lauchter gae he;
    But ere he read it to the end,
       The tear blindit his ee.

5

p. 2   5   'Oh! who is this or who is that,
          Could hae tauld our king o' me
       I wad hae gien him twice as mickle thank
          To hae latten that abe. "

       6   Up an' spak his youngest son
          And the tear blinded his ee'
       'I beg you bide at hame father
          An' I pray you be ruled by me.

       7   For I saw the new mune late yestreen
          Wi' the auld mune in her arms
       O ever an' alake my father dear
          Its a token of a diedly storm"

       8   For I saw the new mune late yestre'en,
          Wi the auld mune in her arms,
       An' ever an alake, my father dear,
          Its a token o' diedly storms."

       9   They hadna sailed a league, a league,
          A league but only three
       When the whirlin' wind, & the ugly jaws
          Cam driving to their knee.

     10   They hadna sailed a league, a league,
          A league but only five,
       When the whirlin' winds and the ugly jaws
          Their gude ship began to rive.

p. 3   11   They hadna sailed a league, a league,
          A league but only nine –
       When the whirlin' wind and the ugly jaws
          Cam driving to their chin.

5   "Oh wha is this, or wha is that
     Has tauld oor king o' me;
   I wad hae gien him twice as muckle thank,
     To latten that abee.'

6   But eat an' drink, my merrie young men,
     Eat an' be weel forn –
   For blaw it wind, or blaw it weet,
     Oor gude ship sails the morn.

7   Up it spak his youngest son,   f. 4ᵛ
     Sat by Sir Patrick's knie.
   "I beg you bide at hame father,
     An' I pray be ruled by me

8   For I saw the new mune late yestre'en,
     Wi the auld mune in her arms,
   An' ever an alake, my father dear,
     Its a token o' diedly storms."

9   "Its eat an' drink, my merrie young men,
     Eat an' be weel forn,
   For blaw it wind, or blaw it weet –
     O'or gude ship sails the morn."

10 They hadna sailed a league, a league,
     A league but only three,
   When the whirlin wind, an' the ugly jaws,
     Cam drivin to their knie.

11 They hadna sailed a league, a league,
     A league but only five,
   Whan the whirlin wind, an' the ugly jaws,
     Their gude ship began to rive.

12 They hadna sailed a league, a league,
     A league but only nine;
   Whan the whirlin winds an' the ugly jaws,
     Cam drivin to their chin.

12   "Oh whaur will I get a bonnie boy
      That will tak the steer in hand?
  Till I gae up to the tap mast
      To look out for dry land."

13   "Oh here am I a bonnie boy
      That will tak the steer in hand
  Till ye gang up to our top mast
      To look out for dry land."

14   He's gane up to the tap mast
      To the tap mast so hie
  He luikit around on ilka side
      But dry land he couldna see.

15   He luikit on his youngest son
      An' the tear blinded his ee'
  "I wish you had been in your mothers bour
      But there you'll never be."

16   Pray for your sells my merry young men
      Pray for yoursells and me
  For the first landin' that we will land,
      Will be in the bottom o' the sea.

p. 4   17   Then up she raise the mermaiden
      Wi the comb and glass in her hand.
  'Here's a health to you my merry young men,
      For you never will see dry land.'

18   O laith, laith were our gude Scots Lords
      To weet their *cork heeld shoon   * or Laigh heele'd
  But lang, lang or the play was pl'ayed,
      Their yellow locks soomed aboon

19   Its och, och ower to Aberdour
      Its fifty fathoms deep –
  And there lie a' our gude Scots Lords
      Wi' Sir Patrick at their feet.

13   "Oh! whaur will I get a bonnie boy,
          Will tak the steer in hand,
      Till I mount up to oor tapmast,
          To luik oot for dry land?"

14   'Oh here am I a bonnie boy,   f. 5ʳ
          Will tak the steer in hand;
      Till you mount up to oor tapmast
          To luik oot for dry land.'

15   He's gaen up to the tapmast,
          To the tapmast sae hie.
      He luikit around on every side,
          But dry land he couldna see.

16   He luikit on his youngest son,
          An the tear blindit his ee,
      Says "I wish you had been in your mother's bowr
          But there you'll never be –

17   Pray for yoursels, my merrie young men,
          Pray for yoursels an' me,
      For the first landen, that we will land,
          Will be in the boddam o' the sea."

18   Then up it raise the mermaiden,
          Wi the comb an' glass in her hand,
      "Here's a health to you my merrie young men,
          For you never will see dry land."

19   Oh! laith, laith waur our gude Scots lords,
          To weet their corkheeled shoon,
      But lang, lang ere the play was played –
          Their yellow locks soomed aboun –

20   There was Saturday, and Sabbathday
          And Monnanday at morn,
      That silken sheets and feather beds,
          Cam floatin' to Kinghorn.

21   O lang, lang will his lady sit
          Wi the fan into her hand
      Afore she see Sir Patrick Spens
          Come sailing to dry land.

22   O lang, lang will his lady sit
          Wi the black shoon on her feet
      Afore she see Sir Patrick Spens
          Come driving up the street.

p. 5   23   O lang, lang will his lady sit
          Wi the saut tear in her ee'
      Afore she see Sir Patrick Spens
          Come hieing to Dundee

20   There was Saturday, an' Sabbathday
     An' Monnonday at morn,
   That feather beds an' silken sheets
     Cam floatin to Kinghorn.

21   It's och, och owre to Aberdour,   f. 5ᵛ
     Its fifty faddoms deep;
   An' there lie a' oor gude Scots Lords,
     Wi' Sir Patrick at their feet.

22   O lang, lang will his lady sit,
     Wi the fan into her hand,
   Until she see her ain dear lord,
     Come sailin to dry land.

23   Oh! lang, lang will his lady sit,
     Wi the tear into her ee.
   Afore she see her ain dear lord
     Come hieing to Dundee.

24   O lang, lang will his Lady sit,
     Wi the black shoon on her feet,
   Afore she see Sir Patrick Spens,
     Come drivin up the street.

2

Sir Colin
[Child no. 61 Sir Cawline]

1   The king luikit ower his castle wa'
      To his nobles ane an a'
    Says "Where it is him Sir Colin,
      I dinna see him among you a'."

2   Up an spak an eldern knicht,
      Aye and even up spak he,
    'Sir Colin's sick for your dochter Janet
      He's very sick, and like to dee.'

3   Win up, win up, my dochter Janet
      I wat you are a match most fine,
    Tak the baken bread, and the wine so red
      And to Sir Colin you maun gang.

4   Up arose that Fair Janet,
      And I wat weel she was na sweer –
    And up arose her merry maries –
      And they said a' they wad gang wi' her.

2

Sir Colin   (Mrs Harris)
[Child no. 61 Sir Cawline]

f. 41^r
no. 12

1   The king luikit owre his castle wa',   f. 5^v
        To his nobles ane an' a.'   no. 2
     Says, "Whare it is him Sir Colin,
        I dinna see him amang you a."

2   Up it spak an eldern knicht;
        Aye an' even, up spak he.
     'Sir Colin's sick for your dochter Janet
        He's very sick, an' like to dee.'

3   "Win up, win up, my dochter Janet,   f. 6^r
        I wat ye are a match most fine;
     Tak the baken bread an' wine sae ried,
        An' to Sir Colin ye maun gieng."

4   Up she rase, that fair Janet –
        An' I wat weel she was na sweer.
     An' up they rase, her merrie Maries;
        An' they said a' they wad gae wi' her.

5   "Oh no, said Fair Janet
     Oh no such things can be
   For a thrang to go to a sick man's bour –
     I think it wad be great folie."

p. 6   6   Hou is my knight all last night?"
     'Very sick, and like to dee,
   But if I had a kiss o' your sweet lips
     I will lie nae langer here.'

7   She leaned her down on his bedside
     I wat she gae him kisses three,
   But wi' sighin' said that Fair Janet
     "As for your bride I daurna be.

8   Unless you watch the Orlange hill,
     And at that hill there grows a thorn
   There ne'er cam a livin man from it,
     Since the first night that I was born."

9   'Oh! I will watch the Orlange hill –
     Tho' I were thinkin to be slain,
   But I will give you some love tokens –
     In case we never meet again.'

10   He gae her rings to her fingers,
     So did he ribbons to her hair,
   He gae her a brooch to her breast bane
     In case they never should meet mair.

11   She put her hand in her pocket;
     And she took out a lang, lang brand –
   "As lang's any man this brand sall keep,
     There shall not a drop of his blood be drawn."

p. 7   12   When ee'n was come, and ee'n bells rung
     I, and a' man bound for bed –
   There beheld him Sir Colin
     Fast to the Orlange hill he rade –

5　　'No, no' said fair Janet,
　　　　No, no such thing can be;
　　　For a thrang to gae to a sick man's bour,
　　　　I think it wald be great folie.'

6　　"How is my knicht, all last nicht?
　　　　'Verie sick an' like to dee,
　　　But if I had a kiss o' your sweet lips.
　　　　I wald lie nae langer here.

7　　She leant her doon on his bedside,
　　　　I wat she gae him kisses three –
　　　But wi sighen said that fair Janet.
　　　　"As for your bride I daurna be.

8　　Unless you watch the Orlange Hill,
　　　　An' at that hill, there grows a thorn;
　　　There ne'er cam a liven man frae it,
　　　　Sin the first nicht, that I was born."

9　　"Oh! I will watch the Orlange hill,
　　　　Though I waur thinkin to be slain,
　　　But I will gie you some love tokens
　　　　In case we never meet again.'

10　　He gae her rings to her fingers,　　　　f. 6ᵛ
　　　　Sae did he ribbons to her hair,
　　　He gae her a broach to her briest bane,
　　　　For fear that they sud ne'er meet mair.

11　　She put her hand in her pocket,
　　　　An' she took oot a lang, lang wand,
　　　"As lang's ony man this wand sall keep;
　　　　There sall not a drap o' his blude be drawn'

12　　Whan ee'n was come, an, ee'n bells rung,
　　　　I an' a' man boun for bed;
　　　There beheld him Sir Colin,
　　　　Fast to the Orlange hill he rade.

13   The wind blew them out at the root,
       So did it auld castles down –
    T'was enough to frighten ony Christian knight
       To be so far frae any town.

14   He rode up – so did he down –
       He rode even thro' the loan –
    Till he spied a knicht wi a lady bricht
       Wi a bent bow into his hand.

15   She cried afar, or she came naur
       "I warn you kind sir, I rede you free
    That for the love you bear to me
       I warn you kind sir that you flee"

16   They fought up, so did they down
       They foucht even thro' the loan
    Till he cut aff the king's richt hand
       Was set about wi chains o' gowd.

17   Haud your hand now Sir Colin
       I wat you've dung my love richt sair,
    But for the love you bear to me
       See that you ding my love nae mair.

p. 8   18   He woo'd, he woo'd that Fair Janet –
       He woo'd her, and he brocht her hame
    He woo'd, he woo'd that Fair Janet
       And ca'ed her Dear Coft to her name

13   The wind blew trees oot at the rutes,
         Sae did it Auld Castles doon –
      T'was eneuch to fricht, ony Christian knicht,
         To be sae far frae ony toon.

14   He rade up, sae did he doon,
         He rade even through the loan;
      Till he spied a knicht, wi' a ladie bricht,
         Wi a bent bow intil his han'.

15   "She cried afar, ere she cam naur,
         I warn ye kind sir, I rede ye free,
      That for the love you bear to me,
         I warn ye kind sir, that ye flee."

16   They faucht up, sae did they doon,
         They faucht even through the loan,
      Till he cut aff the King's richt han'
         Was set aboot wi' chains a' goud.

17   "Haud your hand now Sir Colin,   f. 7ʳ
         I wat you've dung my love richt sair;
      Noo for the love ye bear to me,
         See that ye ding my love nae mair."

18   He wooed, he wooed that fair Janet,
         He wooed her, and he brocht her hame,
      He wooed, he wooed that fair Janet; –
         An' ca'd her, Dear-Coft till her name.

3

Archerdale
[Child no. 47 Proud Lady Margaret]

There cam a Knicht to Arch - er - dale His steed was— win- ders sma, An'

there he spied a La - dy bricht, Look- in' ower— her— Cas - tle wa.

1   There cam a knicht to Archerdale
      His steed was wondr'ous sma'
    And there he spied a lady bricht,
      Lookin' oer her Castle wa'.

2   "You dinna seem a gentle knicht,
      Tho' on horseback you do ride –
    You seem to be some souters son
      You'r boots they are sae wide."

3   'You dinna seem a lady gay –
      Tho' you be bound wi' pride,
    Else you'd let me gae by your fathers gate
      Without either taunt or gibe.'

4   He turned aboot his high horse head
      And away he was bound to ride,
    While neatly with her mouth she spoke,
      "O bide, fine squire oh bide,

3

f. 39[r]
no. 1

1   There cam a knicht to Archerdale,   f. 7[r]
     His steed was winder sma'.   no. 3
    An' there he spied a ladie bricht,
     Luikin owre her Castle wa'.

2   "Ye dinna seem a gentle knicht,
     Though on horseback ye do ride:
    Ye seem to be some sutors son,
     You're butes they are sae wide."

3   'Ye dinna seem a ladie gay,
     Though ye be bound wi' pride –
    Else I'd gane bye your father's gate,
     But either taunt or gibe.'

4   He turned aboot his hie horse head,
     An' awa' he was boun to ride,
    But neatly wi' her mouth she spak,
     "Oh! bide fine squire oh! bide.

5   Bide oh bide, you hindy squire
     Tell me more o' your tale –
    Tell me some o' that unco leed
     You've learned in Archerdale.

p. 9   6   'What gaes in a speul," she said,
     "What in a horn green,
    And what gaes on Lady's head
     When it is washen clean?"

7   'Ale gaes in a speul,' he said
     Wine in a horn green,
    And silk gaes on a lady's head
     When it is washen clean."

8   Aboot he turned his high horse head,
     And away he was bound to ride, –
    When neatly with her mouth she spoke
     "Oh bide fine squire oh bide.

9   Bide oh! bide, you hindy squire
     Tell me more o' youre tale –
    Tell me some o' that unco lied
     You've learned in Archerdale.'

10   You are as like my ae brother
     As ever I did see
    But he's been buried in yon kirkyard,
     Its mair than years are three."

11   I am as like your ae brother
     As ever you did see
    But I canna get peace into my grave
     A' for the pride o' thee.

p. 10   12   Leave pride Janet, leave pride Janet,
     Leave pride and vanitie;
    If you come the roads that I hae come,
     Sair warned will you be.

5   Bide oh bide, ye hindy squire,
      Tell me mair o' your tale –
    Tell me some o' that wondrous lied,
      Ye've learnt in Archerdale.

6   "What gaes in a speal," she said   f. 7ᵛ
      "What in a horn green,
    An' what gaes on a lady's head
      Whan it is washen clean? "

7   'Ale gaes in a speal', he said,
      'Wine in a horn green,
    An' silk gaes on a lady's head,
      Whan it is washen clean.'

8   Aboot he turned his high horse head,
      An' awa' he was boun to ride,
    When neatly wi her mouth she spak,
      Oh bide fine squire oh bide.

9   Bide oh bide ye hindy squire,
      Tell me mair o' your tale.
    Tell me some o' that unco lied,
      You've learnt in Archerdale.

10   Ye are as like my ae brither,
      As ever I did see;
    But he's been buried in yon kirkyaird,
      Its mair than years is three. "

11   'I am as like your ae brither,
      As ever ye did see,
    But I canna get peace into my grave;
      A' for the pride o' thee.

12   Leave pride Janet, leave pride Janet,
      Leave pride an' vanitie:–
    If ye come the roads, that I hae come;
      Sair warnèd will ye be.

13   You come in by Archerdale,
        Wi the gowd plaits in your sleeve,
    When you come in to yon kirkyard,
        You'll gie them a' their leave.

14   You come in by Archer-dale
        Wi the gowd preens in your hair.
    When you come into yon kirkyaird
        You maun them a' forbear –'

15   He got her in her in her mothers bour
        Puttin' gowd knives in her hair –
    He left her [in her] father's garden
        Mournin' for her sins sae sair.

4

Sweet Willie
[Child no. 256 Alison and Willie]

1   My luve she lives in Lincolnshire
        An' I wat she's niether black nor brown;
    But her hair is like the threads o gow'd,
        Aye an it were weel kaimèd down.

13   'Ye come in by yonder kirk,
        Wi' the goud preens in your sleeve;
      When youre brocht hame to yon kirkyaird,
        You'll gie them a' thier leave.

14   'Ye come in to yonder kirk,   f. 8^r
        Wi the goud plaits in your hair;
      When youre brocht hame to yon kirkyaird,
        You will them a' forbear.'

15   He got her in her mither's bour,
        Puttin goud plaits in her hair;
      He left her in her father's gairden,
        Mournin' her sins sae sair.

4

My luve she lives in Lincolnshire   (Mrs Harris)
  [Child no. 256 Alison and Willie]

f. 39^v

no. 4

1   My luve she lives in Lincolnshire;   f. 18^v
       I wat she's niether black nor broun.   no. 13
     But her hair is like the threads o' Gowd
       Aye an' it waur weel kaimèd doun.

2   She pued the black mask oer her face,
      And blinkit gayly wi her ee'.
    "Oh will you to my weddin' come
      And will you bear me gude companie?"

p. 11   3   'I winna to your weddin' come
      Nor will I bear you gude companie,
    Unless you be the bride yoursel,
      An' me the bonnie bridegroom to be.'

4   For me to be the bride mysel
      And you the bonnie bridgroom to be
    Cheer up your heart sweet Willie," she said,
      For that's the day you'll never see."

. . . .

5   He saw a hart draw to a hare,
      And aye that hare drew near a toun,
    And that same hart did get a hare,
      But the gentle knicht got ne'er a toun.

6   He leaned him o'er his saddle bow –
      An' his heart did brak in pieces three
    Wi' sighin said that sweet Willie –
      The pains o' love hae tane hold o me.

. . . .

7   There came a white horse and a letter
      That stopt the weddin speedilie.

2   She's pued the black mask owre her face –
          An' blinkit gaily wi her ee'
       "Oh! will you to my weddin come,
          "An' will you bear me gude companie."

3   'I winna to your weddin come,
          'Nor [will] I bear you gude companie.
       'Unless you be the bride yoursell,
          'An' me the bridegroom to be."

4   "For me to be the bride mysel'   f. 19ʳ
          "An' you the bonnie bridegroom to be –
       "Cheer up your heart, sweet Willie," she said,
          "For that's the day you'll never see –"

5   "Gin you waur on your saiddle set
          "An' gaily ridin on the way –
       "You'll hae nae mair mind o' Alison –
          "Than she waur dead an' laid in clay."

6   When he was on his saiddle set
          An' slowly ridin on the way
       He had mair mind o' Alison –
          Than he had o' the licht o' day.

7   He saw a hart draw near a hare,
          An' aye that hare drew near a toun
       An' that same hart did get a hare,
          But the gentle knicht got neir a toun.

8   He leant him owre his saiddle bow,
          An' his heart did brak in pieces three –
       Wi sighen said him sweet Willie,
          The pains o' luve hae ta'en hald o' me.

                    · · · · · · · · · ·

9   There cam a white horse an' a letter,
          That stopped the weddin speidilie –

25

8   She leaned her head to her bed side
            And her heart did brak in pieces three
      She was buried, and bemoaned,
            But the birds were Willies companie.

5

p. 12   There Were three Ladies
                    [Child no. 11 The Cruel Brother]

1   There were three Ladies in a ha',
            Hech, hey and the lily gay
      By cam a knicht, and he wooed them a'.
            An' the rose is aye the redder aye.

2   The first ane she was clad in green,
            Hech hey &c –
      Will you fancy me and be my queen?
            An' the rose &c

3   You may seek me frae my father dear,
            Hech hey &c
      Or frae my mither, wha did me bear.
            An' the rose &c

10 She leant her back on her bedside
    An' her heart did brak in pieces three –
  She was buried an' bemoaned –
    But the birds waur Willie's companie.

5

There waur Three Ladies (Mrs Harris)
[Child no. 11 The Cruel Brother]

f. 41^r

no. 13

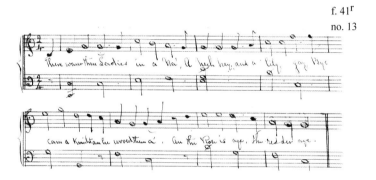

1 There waur three Ladies in a ha'   f. 11^v
    Hech hey, an' the Lily gey,   no. 7
  By cam a knicht an' he wooed them a',
    An' the Rose is aye the redder aye.

2 The first ane she was cled in green,
    Hech hey, an' the lily gey,
  "Will you fancy me an' be my queen?"
    An' the Rose is aye the redder aye.

3 'You may seek me frae my father dear;
    Hech hey an' the lily gey,
  'An' frae my mither wha did me bear,
    An' the Rose is aye the redder aye.

4   Ye may seek me frae my sister Anne,
    Hech hey &c
But no' no, no, frae my brother John –
    An' the rose &c

5   The next ane she was clad in yellow,
    Hech hey &c
Will you fancy me, and be my marrow?
    An the rose &c

6   You may seek me frae my father dear,
    Hech hey &c
Or frae my mither wha did me bear –
    An' the rose &c

7   Ye may seek me frae my sister Anne
    Hech hey &c
But no, no, no, frae my brother John
    An the Rose &c

p. 13   8   The next ane she was clad in red,
    Hech hey &c
Will you fancy me and be my bride?
    An' the Rose &c

9   You may seek me frae my father dear,
    Hech hey &c
Or frae my mither wha did me bear.
    An' the rose &c

10   You may seek me frae my sister Anne.
    Hech hey &c
An' dinna forget my brither John –
    An' the rose &c

11   He sought her frae her father dear,
    Hech hey &c
And frae her mither wha did her bear,
    An the rose, &c

4   'You may seek me frae my sister Anne,
        Hech hey an' the lily gey,
     'But no, no, no frae my brother John,'
        An the Rose is aye the redder aye.

5   The niest ane she was cled in yellow,
        Hech hey an' the lillie gey
     "Will you fancy me, an' be my marrow?"
        An' the Rose is aye the redder aye.

6   'Ye may seek me frae my father dear,
        Hech hey an' the lillie gey.
     'An' frae my mither wha did me bear,
        An' the Rose is aye the redder aye –

7   'Ye may seek me frae my sister Anne' –
        Hech hey an' the lillie gey,
     'But no, no, no frae my brither John' –
        An' the Rose is aye the redder aye –

8   The niest ane she was cled in Red,   f. 12ʳ
        Hech hey, an' the lillie gey,
     "Will ye fancy me, an' be my bride?"
        An' the rose is aye the redder aye.

9   'Ye may seek me frae my father dear,
        Hech hey, an' the lillie gey,
     'An' frae my mither wha did me bear,'
        An' the Rose is aye the redder aye.

10   'Ye may seek me frae my sister Anne,
        Hech hey an' the lillie gey –
     'An' dinna forget my brither John –,
        An' the Rose is aye the redder aye.

11   He socht her frae her father the king,
        Hech hey, an' the lillie gey,
     An' he socht her frae her mither the queen,
        An' the Rose is aye the redder aye.

12   He sought her frae her sister Ann,
            Hech hey &c
        But he forgot her brither John.
            An the rose &c

13   Her mither, she put on her goun –
            Hech hey &c
        And her sister Ann prinned the ribbons doun.
            An' the rose &c

14   Her father, led her doun the close,
            Hech hey &c
        An' her brither John set her on her horse.
            An' the rose &c

p. 14   15   Up and spak the foremost man,
            Hech hey &c
        I think our bonnie bride's pale & wan –
            An' the rose &c

                . . . .

16   What, will you leave to your father dear?
            Hech hey &c
        My . . . . . . and ivory chair
            An' the rose &c

17   What will you leave to your mither dear?

                . . . .

18   What will you leave to your Sister Ann?
            Hech hey &c
        My silken snood, & my golden fan.
            An' the rose &c

12   He socht her frae her sister Anne,
         Hech hey, an' the lillie gey,
      But he forgot her brither John,
         An' the rose is aye the redder aye.

13   Her mither she put on her goun,
         Hech hey, an' the lillie gey,
      An' her sister Anne preened the ribbons doun,
         An' the rose is aye the redder aye.

14   Her father led her doon the close,
         Hech hey, an the lillie gey,
      An' her brither John set her on her horse,
         An' the rose is aye the redder aye.

              . . . .

15   Up an' spak our foremost man,
         Hech hey, an' the lillie gey,   f. 12$^\text{V}$
      "I think oor bonnie bride's pale an' wan"
         An' the rose is aye the redder aye.

              . . . .

16   "What will ye leave to your father dear,?"
         Hech hey an' the lillie gey,
      'My   an my   chair.'
         An' the rose is aye the redder aye."

17   "What will ye leave to your mither dear,?"
         Hech hey, an' the lillie gey –
      'My silken screen I was wont to wear.'
         An' the rose is aye the redder aye.

18   "What will you leave to your sister Anne,?"
         Hech hey, an' the lillie gey,
      'My silken snood, an' my golden fan.'
         An' the rose is aye the redder aye.

19   What will you leeve to your brither John?
       Hech hey &c
The gallows tree to hang him on.
       An the rose is aye the redder aye.

6

Young Logie
[Child no. 182 The Laird o Logie]

1   Pretty is the story that I hae to tell,
       An' pretty is the praisin' o' itsel,
      And' pretty is the prisoner that our king's tane,
       The rantin' young Laird o' Logie.

2   Has he brunt, or has he slain,
       Or has he done any injurie?
Oh no, no, he's done nothing at all,
       But stown a kiss, frae the Queen's Marie.

19   "What will you leave to your Brither John?"
            Hech hey, an' the lillie gey,
        'The gallows tree to hang him on.'
            An' the rose is aye the redder aye.

6

Young Logie   (Mrs Harris)
[Child no. 182   The Laird o Logie]

f. 42[r]
no. 17

1   Pretty is the story, I hae to tell,   f. 16[r]
            Pretty is the praisin' o' itsel.'   no. 10
        An' pretty is the pris'ner oor King s tane.
            The rantin' young Laird o' Logie.

2   Has he brunt? or has he slain?
            Or has he done any injurie?
        Oh! no, no he's done nothing at all,
            But stown a kiss frae the Queen's Marie.

3   Lady Margaret, cam down the stair,
      Wringing her hands and tearing her hair.
    Crying oh that ever I to Scotland cam,
      Aye to see Young Logie dee.

4   Haud your tongue, now Lady Margaret –
      And a' your weepin' lat abe –
    For I'll gae to the king mysel –
      An' plead for life to Young Logie.

5   First whan I to Scotland cam,
      You promised gie me askens three –
    The first then o' these askens is
      Life for the young Laird o Logie.

6   If you had asked houses or lands
      They should hae been at your command,
    But tomorrow ere I taste meat or drink –
      High hanged shall Young Logie be.

7   Lady Margaret came doun the stair –
      Wringing her hands, and tearing her hair.
    Crying oh! that ever I to Scotland cam,
      Aye to see Young Logie dee.

8   Haud your tongue, now Lady Margaret,
      And a' your weepin lat abe –
    For I'll ge to the king mysel
      And plead for life, for Young Logie.

9   She counterfieted, the king's hand write.
      And stole frae him his richt hand glue
    And sent them to Pitcairn Wa's
      Aye to set Young Logie free.

3   Ladie Margaret cam doon the stair,
       Wringing her hands, an' tearin her hair, –
     Cryin "oh! that ever I to Scotland cam,
       Aye to see Young Logie dee."

4   'Had your tongue, noo lady Margaret;
       'An' a' your weepin' lat a-bee,
     'For I'll gae to the King my sell,
       'An' plead for life to Young Logie.'

5   'First whan I to Scotland cam;   f. 16ᵛ
       'You promised to gie me askens three,
     'The first then o' these asken's is
       'Life for the Young Laird o' Logie.'

6   "If you had askèd houses or lands;
       "They suld hae been at your command;
     "But the morn ere I taste meat or drink,
       "High hangèd sall Young Logie be."

7   Lady Margaret cam doon the stair,
       Wringin her hands, an' tearin' her hair.
     Cryin "oh! that ever I to Scotland cam,
       "A' to see Young Logie dee."

8   'Haud your tongue, noo Lady Margaret,
       'An' a' your weepin lat a bee;
     'For I'll counterfiet the King's hand write,
       'An' steal frae him his richt hand gloe,
     'An' send them to Pitcairn's wa's,
       'A' to lat Young Logie free.'

9   She counterfieted the king's hand write,
       An' stole frae him his richt hand gloe:
     An' sent them to Pitcairn's wa's,
       A' to set Young Logie free.

p. 16   10   The king lookit o'er his Castle wa'
        Was lookin to see what he could see.
      "My life to wade, and my lands to pawn –
        Yonder comes the young Laird o' Logie."

    11   'Pardon, oh pardon my lord the king –
        Aye I pray you, pardon me
      For I counterfieted your hand write,
        And stole frae you your richt hand glue
      And sent them to Pitcairn Wa's
        A' to Let Young Logie free.

    12   "If this had been done by laird, or lord,
        Or by baron of a high degree –
      I'll make him sure, upon my word,
        His life should hae gane for Young Logie.

    13   But since it is my gracious Queen,
        A hearty pardon we will gie.
      And for her sake I'll free the loun,
        The rantin young Laird o' Logie."

10   The King luikit owre his Castle Wa',
         Was luikin to see what he cald see,
      "My life to wad, an' my Land to pawn,
         "Yonder comes the Young Laird o' Logie!"

11   Pardon, oh! pardon My Lord the King;
         Aye I pray you pardon me,"
      For I counterfieted your hand write,
         An' stole frae you, your richt hand gloe,
      'An' sent them to Pitcairn's Wa's,   f. 17ʳ
         'A to set Young Logie free.

12   "If this had been done by laird, or Lord,
         "Or by baron of high degree; –
      "I'se mak it sure, upon my word,
         "His life suld hae gane for Young Logie.'

13   "But since it is my gracious Queen,
         "A hearty pardon we will gie,
      "An, for her sake, we'll free the loon;
         "The rantin' Young Laird o' Logie.

7

Young Reedin
[Child no. 68 Young Hunting]

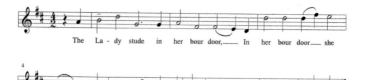

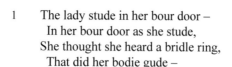

1   The lady stude in her bour door –
      In her bour door as she stude,
    She thought she heard a bridle ring,
      That did her bodie gude –

2   She thought it had been her father dear
      As he cam ridin' hame,
    But it was her true love Reedin'
      Come hiching to her han'.

p. 17   3   "You're welcome, you're welcome young Reedin
      To coal and candle licht –   [she said –
    You're welcome, you're welcome, young Reedin',
      To sleep in my bour this nicht.

4   'I thank you for your coal Madam
      And for your candle too –
    There's a fairer maid at Bridge Water,
      I love better than you."

7

Young Riedan   (Mrs Harris)
[Child no. 68 Young Hunting]

f. 39ᵛ
no. 5

1   The ladie stude in her bour door,   f. 8ʳ
     In her bour door as she stude,   no. 4
    She thocht she heard a bridle ring,
     That did her bodie gude –

2   She thocht it had been her father dear
     Come ridin owre the sand –
    But it was her true love Riedan,
     Come hiean to her hand.

3   "You're welcom, you're welcom young Riedan,
     "To coal an' cannel licht,   [she said,
    "You're welcom, you're welcom young Riedan,
     "To sleep in my bour this nicht."

4   'I thank you for your coal madame,
     'An' for your cannel tae,
    'There's a fairer maid at Clydeswater,
     'I love better than you.'

5   "A fairer maid than me, Reedin'
        A fairer maid than me
     A fairer maid than me Reedin'
        You sure did never see."

6   He leaned him o'er his saddle bow –
        To gie her a kiss sae sweet –
     She keppit him on a little penknife,
        And gae him a wound sae deep.

7   "Oh hide, oh hide my bourswoman,
        Oh hide this deed on me;
     And the silks that were shapit for me at Yule
        At pace shall be sewed for thee."

8   They saddled young Reedin, they bridled young
        In the way he was wont to ride,   [Reedin
     Wi a hunting horn about his neck,
        And a sharp sword by his side –

9   And they are on to Clydiswater,
        And rode it up and down –
     And the deepest linn in Clydiswater,
        They flang him young Reedin.

p. 18   10   Now lie you there, you young Reedin
        Your bed it is fu wan.
     The maid you hae at Bridgewater
        For you she will think lang."

11   Then up an' spak the wily bird,
        As it sat on the tree,
     'Oh woe be to you ill woman
        And an ill death may you dee,
     For he had ne'er anither love,
        Anither love, but thee.'

5   A fairer maid than me, Riedan;   f. 8ᵛ
       A fairer maid than me;
     A fairer maid than ten o' me,
       You shurely ne'er did see!

6   He leant him owre his saidle bow,
       To gie her a kiss sae sweet.
     She keppit him on a little penknife,
       An' gae him a wound sae deep.

7   "Oh! hide, oh! hide my bourswoman,
       Oh! hide this deed on me;
     An' the silks that waur shappit for me at Yule,
       At pasch sall be sewed for thee."

8   They saidled young Riedan, they bridled young
       The way he was wont to ride;   [Riedan
     Wi' a huntin horn aboot his neck;
       An' a sharp sword by his side –

9   An' they are on to Clydeswater
       An' they rade it up & doon –
     An' the deepest linn in a' Clydeswater,
       They flang him – young Riedan.

10   "Lie you there you young Riedan;
       Your bed it is fu' wan;
     The [maid] you hae at Clydeswater,
       For you she will think Lang!"

11   Up it spak, the wily bird,
       As it sat on the tree;
     "Oh wae betide you ill woman,
       "An' an ill death may you dee,
     "For he had nee'r anither love
       "Anither love but thee."

41

12   "Come down, come down my pretty parrot –
      And pickle wheat off my hand
   And your cage shall be o' the beaten gowd,
      When it's o' the willow wand."

13   'I winna come down, and I sanna come down
      To siccan a traitor as thee,
   For as you did to young Reedin,
      Sae wad you do wi' me.'

14   "Come down, come down my pretty parrot,
      And pickle wheat aff my glue,
   And your cage shall be o' the gude red gowd,
      When it's of the willow tree."

15   'I winna come down, I sanna come down
      To siccan a traitor as thee,
   You wad wring the head off my hause bone
      And fling it in the sea.'

16   It fell upon a Lammas tide
      The king's court came ridin bye –
   "Oh where it is him young Reedin,'
      It's fain I w'ad him see."

p. 19

17   'Oh I hae no seen young Reedin
      Sin   at morn –
   It bodes me sair, an dreids me mair,
      Clydes water's him forlorn.'

12   'Come doon, come doon my pretty parrot,   f. 9^r
            'An' pickle wheat aff my glue;
         'An' your cage sall be o' the beaten goud;
            'Whan its' of the willow tree.'

13   "I winna come doon, I sanna come doon,
            "To siccan a traitor as thee;
         "For as you did to young Riedan;
            "Sae wald you do to mee – "

14   'Come doon, come doon my pretty parrot,
            'An' pickle wheat aff my hand;
         'An' your cage sall be 'o the beaten goud,
            'Whan its o' the willow wand.'

15   "I winna come doon, I sanna come doon,
            "To siccan a traitor as thee,
         "You wald thraw my head aff my hasebane,
            "An' fling it in the sea."

16   It fell upon a Lammas tide,
            The King's court cam ridin bye – ;
         "Oh! whare it is him, Young Riedan,
            Its fain I wald him see."

17   'Oh! I hae no seen Young Riedan
            'Sin three lang weeks the morn –
         'It bodes me sair, and driedss me mair,
            'Clydeswater's him forlorn.'

. . . .

18   "Gie up, gie up your day seekin'
      And ye maun siek by nicht
   And on the place youn[g] Reedin lies
      The candles burn bricht."

19   They've gien owre their day seekin
      And they did seek by nicht
   And on the place young Reedin lay,
      The candles burnt'd bricht.

20   The first an' grip his mither got
      Was o' his milk white hand,
   And was na that a dowie grip
      To bring sae far to land?

21   The next an grip his mither got,
      Was o' his yellow hair,
   And was na that a dowie grip,
      To get her ae son there?

22   Oh white, white were his wounds washen
      As white as ony lawn –
   But soon's the traiteress stude before
      Then out the red blude sprang.

. . . .

18   Up it spak the wily bird;
      As it sat on the tree –

. . . .

19   "Leave aff, leave aff your day seekin,   f. 9ᵛ
      "An' ye maun seek by nicht;
    "Aboon the place young Riedan lies,
      "The cannels burn bricht."

20   They gae up their day seekin,
      An' they did seek by nicht;
    An' owre the place young Riedan lay,
      The cannels burnt bricht,

21   The firsten grip his mother got,
      Was o' his yellow hair;
    An' wasna that a dowie grip,
      To get her ae son there?

22   The nexten grip his mother got,
      Was o' his milk-white hand;
    An' was-na that a dowie grip,
      To bring sae far to land?

23   White, white waur his wounds washen,
      As white as ony lawn;
    But sune's the traitor stude afore,
      Then oot the red blude sprang.

. . . .

p. 20 23   Fire wadna tak on her bourswoman,
          On niether cheek nor chin,
        But fast it took on these twa hands,
          That flang young Reedin in.

      24   "Come out, come out my bourswoman
          Come out, lat me win in,
        For as I did the deed mysel –
          Sae I maun drie the pine."

8

Glen Logie
[Child no. 238 Glenlogie, or, Jean o Bethelnie]

      1   There were aucht and forty nobles,
          Rode to the king's ha'
        But bonnie Glen Logie,
          Was the flour o' them a'.

      2   There were aucht and forty nobles,
          Rode to the king's dine,
        But bonnie Glenlogie
          Was the flour o' thrice nine.

      3   Bonnie Jeanie Melville
          Cam trippin doun the stair,
        And when she saw Glen Logie,
          Her heart it grew sair.

      4   "Oh who is that gallant
          And who are his kin?
        'He's of the gay Gordons
          His name it is John.'

24   Fire wadna tak on her bourswoman,
          Niether on cheek nor chin;
      But it took fast on thae twa hands,
          That flang Young Riedan in.

25   "Come oot, come oot my bourswoman,
          "Come oot, lat me win in;
      For as I did the deed my sell,
          Sae man I drie the pine."

8

              There waur Aucht an' forty nobles   (Mrs Harris)
      [Child no. 238 Glenlogie, or, Jean o Bethelnie]
                  Air "Auld Rob Morris"

1   There waur aucht an' forty nobles   f. 17ʳ
          Rade to the king's ha',   no. 11
      But Bonnie Glen logie
          Was the flour o' them a'.

2   There waur aucht an' forty nobles,
          Rade to the king's dine,
      But bonnie Glen logie,
          Was the flour o' thrice nine.

3   Bonnie Jeanie Melville,
          Cam trippin' doun the stair,
      An' whan she saw Glen Logie,
          Her hairt it grew sair.

              . . . .

4   He's of the gay Gordon's
          His name it is John.

                        47

5   "Oh Logie, oh Logie oh Logie " said she
         "If I get na Glenlogie, I surely will dee. "

p. 21   6   He turned him about,
         As the Gordons do a',
      Says, 'I thank you Lady Jeannie,
         But I'm promised awa.'

        7   She called on her maidens
         Her hands for to take
      And the rings from her fingers
         She did them all break.

        8   'Oh haud your tongue my dochter
         Lat your weeping abe
      I'll wed you to Glenfinlas
         He's twice as gude as he.'

        9   "Oh Logie, oh Logie, oh Logie," said she
         If I get na Glen Logie, I surely will dee."

       10   'Oh what is my Lineage,
         Or what is my make?
      That such a fine Lady
         Should dee for my sake?'

       11   Such a pretty weddin as I have been told
      And bonnie Jeannie Melville
      Was scarce sixteen years old.

5   "Oh! Logie, oh! Logie
     'Oh Logie," said she,
    "If I get na Glenlogie,
     "I surely will dee."

6   He turned him aboot   f. 17ᵛ
     As the Gordon's do a',
    Says 'I thank you Lady Jeanie,
     But I'm promised awa.'.

7   She called on her maidens,
     Her hands for to take;
    An' the rings from her fingers,
     She did them a' break.

. . . .

8   'Oh! what is my Lineage?
     'Or what is my make?
    'That such a fine Lady,
     'Suld dee for my sake.?'

. . . .

9   Such a pretty wedding,
     As I have been told;
    An' bonnie Jeanie Melville,
     Was scarce sixteen years old.

9

Roudesdales
[Child no. 246 Redesdale and Wise William]

1   Roudesdales and Clerk William,
        Sat birlin' at the wine,
      And a' the talk was them atween,
        Was aboot the ladies fine.

p. 22   2   Says, "Roudesdales to Clerk William
        "I'll wad my lands wi' thee –
      I'll wad my lands against your head,
        And that is what I'll dee.

3   That there's no a lady in a' the land
        That is fair baith ee' and brie
      Wha I winna wed without courtin,
        Wi' ae blink o' my ee'"

4   Its I hae ae sister dear,
        And she's fair baith ee' & brie,
      And you'll no wed her without courtin'
        Wi ae blink o' your ee.'

            . . . .

5   He has wrote a broad letter,
        Between the nicht and the day,
      And sent it to his ae sister
        Wi the white feather, and the gray.

      He has wrote a broad letter,
        Between the nicht an' the day,

9

Roudesdales   (Mrs Harris)
[Child no. 246 Redesdale and Wise William]
Air "Johnnie Brod"

1   Roudesdales an' Clerk William,   f. 14ᵛ
       Sat birlin at the wine,   no. 9
     An' a' the talk was them atween,
       Was aboot the ladies fine, fine,
       Was aboot the Ladies fine.

2   Says Roudesdales to Clerk William,
        "I'll wad my lands wi' thee;
       "I'll wad my lands against thy head,
        "An' that is what I'll dee. &c.
        &c

3   "That there's no a leddy in a' the land,   f. 15ʳ
        "That's fair baith ee' an' bree;
       "That I winna wed withoot courtin',
        "Wi' ae blink o' my ee." &c

4   'Says William 'I've an ae sister,
        'She's fair baith ee' an' bree;
       'An' you'll no wed her withoot courtin',
        'Wi ae blink o' your ee.'

                · · · · · · · · · ·

5   He has wrote a broad letter,
        Between the nicht an' the day;
      An' sent it to his ae sister,
        Wi' the white feather, an' the gray.

And sent it to his ae sister –,
 Wi' the white feather and the grey.§

6 The first an' line she luikit on
 A licht lauchter gae she –
But ere' she read it to the end
 The tear blinded her ee'.

   . . . .
7   'My ae' brither
Suld wad his head for me "

p. 23 8 Roudesdales to her bour has gone,
 And rode it round about –
And there he spied that fair Lady
 At a window Looking out.

9 'Come down, come down, you fair Lady
 Ae sicht o' you to see,
For the gouns are o' the silks sae fine
 That I will gie to thee.'

10 If your's are o' the silk sae fine
 Mine's o' the bonnie brown –
So get you gone, you Roudesdale,
 For I will no' come down –"

§ Editorial note: This verse has not been numbered since it is evidently a repeat of 5. Writing done with a finer nib than that used for verses 1-5 begins with this verse.

6   The firsten line she luekit on,
       A licht lauchter gae she,
     But e'er she read it to the end,
       The tear blindit her ee.

7   'Oh wae betide my ae brither,
       Wald wad his head for me –'
              . . . .

8   Roudesdales to her bour has gane,
       An' rade it round aboot.,
     An' there he saw that fair ladie,
       At a window lookin oot.

9   "Come doon, come doon you fair ladie,
       "Ae sicht o' you to see,
     "For the rings are o' the goud sae ried;
       "That I will gie to thee."

10   'If your's are o' the goud sae ried;   f. 15$^\text{v}$
       'Mine's o' the silver clear,
     'So get you gone, you Roudesdales,
       'For you sall no be here."

11   "Come doon, come doon you lady fair,
       "Ae sicht o' you to see,
     "For the gouns are o' the silk sae fine,
       "That I will gie to thee.

12   'If your's are o' the silk sae fine,
       'Mine's o' the bonnie broun,
     'Sae get you gone, you Roudesdales,
       'For I will no come doon."

11   'Come doun, come doun you fair Lady,
              Ae sicht o' you to see
          For the rings are o' the gowd sae red,
              That I will gie to thee –

12   "If yours' are o' the gowd sae red
              Mine's o' the silver clear –
          So get you gone you Roudesdales
              For you sall no be here."

13   Come doun, come down, you fair Lady
              Ae sicht o' you to see,
          For the steeds are o' the milk sae white
              That I will gie to thee.'

14   If yours are o' the milk sae white,
              Mine's o' the bonnie broun,
          So get you gone you Roudesdales,
              For I will no come doun –"

p. 24   15   'Come doun, come doun, you fair Lady –
              Ae sicht o' you to see –
          Or I will set your bour on fire,
              Between your nourse an' thee –'

16   "You may set my bour on fire
              And I'm no doubtin' but you'll dee –
          There will come a sharp shower frae the west
              Will slocken it speedilie."

17   He has set her bour on fire,
              And quickly it did flame –
          But there cam a sharp shower frae the west
              That put it out again.

18   Out among the fire and smoke
              That bonnie lady cam,
          Wi' as muckle gowd aboon her brie,
              As wad bought an earldom.

13   "Come doon, come doon you ladie fair,
      "Ae sicht o' you to see,
      "For the steeds are o' the milk sae white,
      "That I will gie to thee."

14   'If yours are o' the milk sae white,
      'Mine's o' the bonnie broun.
      'Sae get you gone you Roudesdales,
      'For I will no come doon.'

15   "Come doon, come doon you ladie fair,
      "Ae sicht o' you to see,
      "Or I will set your bour on fire
      "Atween your nurse an' thee."

16   'You may set my bour on fire,
      'As I doubt-na you will dee,
      'But there'll come a sharp shour, frae the wast
      'Will slocken't speedilie.'

17   He has set her bowr on fire,   f. 16^r
      An' quickly it did flame,
      But there cam a sharp shour frae the wast,
      That put it oot again.

18   Oot amang the fire an' smoke
      That bonnie lady cam –
      Wi' as muckle goud aboon her bree,
      As wald bocht an earldom –

19   'Oh! woe be to you ill woman,
        An ill death mat you dee –
        For you hae won your brother's head,
        And I go landless free.'

10

Johnnie Armstrong
[Child no. 169 Johnie Armstrong]

1   There lived a man, in the north west land
        His name was John Armstrong
        He had niether lands nor rents –
        But he keepit aucht score o' warlike men.

2   The king he wrote a loving letter –
        Wi his ain hand sae tenderlie –
p. 25   And he sent it to John Armstrong,
        To come and speak wi' him speedilie –

19　　"Oh! wae betide you ill woman,
　　　　"An' ill ill died may you dee,
　　　　"For ye hae won your brither's head,
　　　　"An' I go landless free. – "

10

Johnnie Armstrong　　　　(Mrs Harris)
[Child no. 169　Johnie Armstrong]

f. 42^r
no. 19

1　　There lived a man, in the North west land –　f. 25^v
　　　His name was John Armstrong,　　　　　no. 24
　　He had niether land nor rent
　　　But he keepit eight score of warlike men.

2　　The king he wrote a broad letter,
　　　Wi his ain hand sae tenderlie,
　　An' sent it to Johnnie Armstrong,
　　　To come an' speak wi him speedilie.

3   "Now that we must go before the king,
         We will go courageouslie
      For father " he said "nor grandfather
         Either of the two I ne'er did see."

4   He dressed his merry men all in green,
         And he himself in the scarlet red –
      And every man had a milk white steed,
         And hats, and feathers, all alike –

5   When they cam before the king –
         He fell low down on his knee
      The king he moved his hat from his head
         For he thought, he'd been a king as well as he.

6   "Pardon oh! pardon my lord the King,
         Aye I pray you pardon me,
      For my name is John Armstrong,
         I'm subject to the king, my liege," said he.

7   'There is no pardon that thou shalt get.
         There is no mercy for thee
      Tomorrow ere I taste meat or drink
         High hanged shall your eight score of men and
                                    [you be.'

8   He lookit him o'er his left shoulder –
         I wat the tear, blinded his ee'
      Says "we've begged grace at a graceless face,
         For there's niether mercy for you nor me.

9   But we will scorn to die like dogs –
         We'll fight you all courageously
p. 26   If the king had not moved his foot as he did
         I would have ta'en his head from his fair bodie."

3   Now since we must go before the king: f. 26^r
         We will go courageously;
     For father he said nor grandfather,
         Either of the two, I ne'er did see.

4   He dressed his merrie men all in green;
         An' he himself in the Scarlet red.
     An' every man had a milk white steed
         An' hats an' feathers all alike.

5   When they cam before the king,
         He fell low down on his knie.
     The king he movèd his hat from his head,
         For he thought he'd been a king as well as he.

6   "Pardon oh! pardon my lord the king,
         "Aye I pray thee pardon me,
     "For my name is John Armstrong,
         "I'm subject to the king my liege," said he

7   There is no pardon that thou shalt get,
         'There is no mercie for thee
     'To-morrow before I taste meat or drink,
         'High hangèd shall your eight score of men and
                                                    [you be.'

8   He luikit him owre his left shoulder,
         I wat the tear blindit his ee,
     Says, 'we've beggit grace at a graceless face;
         'For there's niether mercy for you nor me.

9   'But we shall scorn to die like dogs,
         'We'll fight you all courageously
     'If the king had not movèd his foot as he did,
         'I would have taen his head, from his fair bodie.'

10   But had I kenned ere I cam fram hame,
         How thou unkind would hae been to me;
     I wald hae keepit the border side,
         In spite of all your force an' thee.

10   They fought up, so did they down –
      They fought on most gallantlie
    Till they left not a man in the king s lifegaurd,
      Never a man but barely three –

11   Edinburgh city it rose up,
      It rose up by thousands three
    Till a cowardly man, came John behind,
      And run him through his fair bodie.

12   "Fight on, fight on, my merry men
      I am a little hurt but I am not slain
    So here I'll lie and bleed a while
      And rise and fight with you again."

13   They took the gallows frae the glack
      And there they set it on a plain –
    And there they hanged Johnnie Armstrong
      Wi' fifty of his warlike men.

14   His lady lookit oe'r her tour sae high
      Aye to see what she could see
    And there she spied a pretty little boy –
      Was comin riding speedilie.

15   'What news, what news, my pretty little boy
      Aye what news have you to me.'
    I have no news said the pretty little boy,
      "But Johnnie Armstrong thou shalt never see."

16   If this be true my pretty little boy –
      Aye the news you tell to me
    You'll be the heir of a' my lands –
      You and your young son after thee.'

11   Edinborrow city it rose up
      It rose up by thousands three
    Till they left not a man in the king's life gaurd;
      Never a man, but barely three.

12   They fought up, so did they doun;   f. 26ᵛ
      They fought on most gallantly:
    Till a cowardly man, cam John behind,
      And run him through his fair bodie.

13   They took the gallows frae the glack,
      An' there they set it on a plain,
    An' there they hanged Johnnie Armstrong,
      Wi fifty of his warlike men.

14   His ladie luikit oure her castle wa,
      Was luikin to see what she could see
    An' there she spied a bonny little boy,
      Comin ridin speedilie.

15   "What news, what news my pretty little boy,
      "Aye what news have ye to me? "
    'I have no news," said the pretty little boy
      But Johnnie Armstrong you'll never see.'

16   "If that be true my pretty little boy,
      "Aye the news you tell to me,
    "You'll be the hier of a' my lands
    "You an' your young son after thee."

11

p. 27

The Earl o' Roslyn's Dochter
[Child no. 46 Captain Wedderburn's Courtship]

O I maun hae to my sup-per, a— bird with-out a bone.— An' I maun hae to my sup-per, A cher-ry with-out a stone; A spar-row's horn, a priest un-born, This nicht shall join—us twa,— Be-fore that I go with you, I tell you aye, or no.

1   The Earl o' Roslyns dochter,
      Gaed out ae nicht in spring,
      She met wi Captain Wedderburn
      A servant to the king –

. . . .

11

Captain Wedderburn   (Mrs Harris)
[Child no. 46 Captain Wedderburn's Courtship]

f. 41ᵛ
no. 15

1   The Earl o' Roslin s dochter,   f. 19ᵛ
      Gaed oot to tak the air,   no. 14
     She met a gallant gentleman;
      As hame she did repair.

. . . .

2   I will tak you wi me,
      I tell you aye or no.

. . . .

2   Haud far awa frae me kind sir –
        Haud far awa frae me.

. . . .

3   Supper bell it will be rung,
        And I'll be missed awa',

. . . .

4   Questions six you'll answer me
        And that is four and twa –
        Before that I go with you,
          I tell you aye or na.

. . . .

5   What's   than woman's wishes,
        What's deeper than the sea?

. . . .

6   I maun hae to my supper
        A bird without a bone,
        And I maun hae to my supper,
         A cherry without a stone.

p. 28   7   I maun hae a gentle bird,
        That flies without a ga' –
        Before that I gae with you
         I tell you aye or na.

3   I am Captain Wedderburn
      A servant to the king.

            . . . .

4   I will tak you wi me
      I tell you aye or no.

5   'I maun hae to my supper,
       'A bird without a bone,
      'An' I maun hae to my supper
       'A cherry without a stone –

6   'An' I maun hae a gentle bird,
       'That flies withoot a ga'
      'Before that I gae with you,
       'I tell you aye or na –

8   I maun hae some winter fruit,
       That in December grew –
     And I maun hae a gay mantle,
       That waft has ne'er ca'd through –

9   A sparrow's horn, a priest unborn
       This nicht to join us twa –
     Before that I go with you,
       I tell you aye or na – "

10   'When the bird is in the egg –
       I'm sure it has no bone,
     And when the cherry's in the bud,
       I'm sure it has no stone.

11   The dove it is a gentle bird,
       It flies without a ga'
     So I will tak you with me
       I tell you aye or na.'

12   The priest is standing at the gate
       Just ready to come in,
     No man can say that he was born
       No man without a sin.

. . . .

p. 29   13   So I will tak you with me
       I tell you aye or na –

7 'I maun hae some winter fruit,
   'That in December grew
'An' I maun hae a gey mantle,
   'That waft was ne'er ca'ed through –

8 'A sparrow's horn, a priest unborn
   'This nicht to join us twa –
'Afore that I go with you
   'I tell you aye or na.'

9 "When the bird is in the egg,   f. 20^r
   "I'm sure it has nae bone –
"An' when the cherry is in the bud,
   "I'm sure it has nae stone.

10 "The dove it is a gentle bird,
   "It flies without a ga'
"Sae I will tak you with me,
   "I tell you aye or na –

11 "My father has some winter fruit
   "That in December grew,
"My mother has a gey mantle,
   "That waft was nee'r ca'd through –

12 "A sparrow's horn you sune sall get
   "There's one on every claw –
"Sae I will tak you with me
   "I tell you aye or na –

13 The priest is standing at the gate,
   "Just ready to come in –
"Nae man can say that he was born –
   "Nae man without a sin –

       . . . .

14 "Sae I will tak you with me
   "I tell you aye or no."

14   My father has some winter fruit
           That in December grew
         My mother has a gay mantle
           That waft has ne'er ca'd through –

15   A sparrow's horn you soon shall get
           There's one on every claw;
         So I will tak you with me
           I tell you aye or na.'

12

The Rose o' Balindie
[Child no. 20 The Cruel Mother]

Oh fause Moth - er, when we war thine, Hey for the Rose o' Ma - lin - die O Ye

did - na feed us wi the flour bread an wine, A' - down by the green wood Si - die O.

1   She leaned her back against a thorn
         It's hey for the Rose o' Balindie O,
       And there she has twa bonnie babes born
         Adown by the green wood sidie O.

12

The Rose o' Malindie O   (Mrs Harris &
[Child no. 20 The Cruel Mother]   others)

1   She leant her back against a thorn   f. 10^r
      Hey for the Rose o' Malindie O,   no. 5
     And there she has twa bonnie babes born –
      Adoon by the green wood Sidie O.

2 She's ta'en the garter frae her leg,
   It's hey for the Rose o' Balindie O!
  And hangit their necks till they were dead –
   Adown by the green wood sidie O.

3 She lookit out owre her castle wa'
   Its hey for the Rose o' Balindie O.
  And saw twa bonnie boys playin at the ba',
   Adown by the green wood sidie O!

4 Oh! bonnie babes if you were mine –
   It's hey for the Rose o' Balindie O.
p. 30 I would feed you wi' the flour bread & wine
   Adown by the green wood sidie O."

5 'Oh! fause mother when we were thine
   Its hey for the Rose o' Balindie O –
  You didna feed us wi' the flour bread & wine
   Adown by the green wood sidie O.

6 You took the garter frae your leg –
   Its hey for the Rose o' Balindie O
  And hangit our necks till we were dead,
   Adown by the green wood sidie O.

7 You sall be seven years fish in the sea,
   Its hey for the Rose o' Balindie O.
  And you sall be seven years bird on the tree,
   Adown by the green wood sidie O.

2   She's taen the Ribbon, frae her head –
      Hey for the Rose o' Malindie O,!
    An' hankit their necks till they waur dead:
      Adoon by the greenwude sidie O.

3   She luikit outowre her castle wa'
      Hey for the Rose o' Malindie O!
    An' saw twa nakit boys, playin at the ba',
      Adoon by the greenwude sidie O

4   "Oh! bonnie boys waur ye but mine;–
      "Hey for the Rose o' Malindie O,
    "I wald feed ye wi flour bread an' wine,
      "Adoon by the greenwude sidie O."

5   'Oh fause mother whan we waur thine;
      Hey for the Rose o' Malindie O,
    'Ye didna feed us wi' flour bread & wine',
      'Adoon by the greenwude sidie O.'

6   "Oh! bonnie boys gif ye waur mine,
      Hey for the Rose o' Malindie O,
    "I wald clied ye, wi silk sae fine,
      "Adoon by the greenwude sidie O."

7   Oh! fause mother, whan we waur thine;
      Hey for the Rose o' Malindie O,
    "You didna clied us in silk sae fine,
      'Adoon by the greenwude sidie O.'

8   'Ye tuik the Ribbon aff your head;   f. 10^{v}
      Hey for the Rose o' Malindie O,
    'An' hankit our necks till we waur dead –
      'Adoon by the greenwude sidie O.'

9   'You sall be seven years bird on the tree,
      Hey for the Rose o' Malindie O.
    'Ye sall be seven years fish in the sea,
      'Adoon by the greenwude sidie O,

8   You sall be seven years eel in the pool,
         Its hey for the Rose o' Balindie O.
        And you sall be seven years down into hell
         Adown by the green wood sidie O.

9   "Welcome, welcome fish in the sea –
         Its hey for the Rose o' Balindie O –
        An' welcome, welcome, bird on the tree
         Adown by the green wood sidie O.

10   Welcome, welcome eel in the pool –
         Its hey for the Rose o Balindie O –
        But oh! for Heaven's sake keep me out o hell –
         Adown by the green wood sidie O.' "

13

p. 31

Johnnie Brod
[Child no. 114 Johnnie Cock]

John - nie Brod in a May morn - in', Got___ wa - ter for his___ hands, An' he ca'd on his___ twa bluid hounds, Waur___ bound wi i - ron bands, bands, waur___ bound wi i - ron bands.

10   'Ye sall be seven years eel in the pule,
           'Hey for the Rose o' Malindie O!
         'An' ye sall be seven years doon into Hell,
           'Adoon by the greenwude sidie O.'

11   "Welcome, welcome bird on the tree,
           Hey for the Rose o' Malindie O,
         'Welcome welcome fish i the sea;
           "Adoon by the greenwude sidie O.

12   Welcome, welcome eel i' the pule,
           Hey for the Rose o' Malindie O!
         "But oh! for gudesake keep me frae hell,
           "Adoon by the greenwude sidie O!"

13

Johnnie Brod   (Mrs Harris)
[Child no. 114   Johnnie Cock]

f. 42^r
no. 18

13 Johnnie Brod

1   Johnnie Brod on a May morning
      Called for water to his hands
    And he's let out his twa bloud hounds
      Were bound wi' iron bands.

2   He has made a solemn aith
      Atween the sun and the mune
    That he wad on to the gude green wood
      The dun deer to ding doun.

3   Up and spak Johnnie s mither
      And a wae, wae woman was she –
    I beg you bide at hame Johnnie
      And I pray you be ruled by me.

4   Baken bread you shall na want
      And wine you shall lack nane –
    Now Johnnie for my benison
      I beg you bide at hame.

5   . . . .
      Advice he wad take nane
    He strippit himsel o' the scarlet red
      And put on the licht Lincoln-green.

. . . .

6   He luikit east, he luikit west.
      And in below the sun –

13 Johnnie Brod

1   Johnnie Brod, on a May mornin,
         Called for water to wash his hands,
      An' there he spied his twa blude hounds,
         Waur bound in iron bands, bands,
         Waur bound in iron bands.

2   Johnnie s ta'en his gude bent bow –
         Bot an' his arrows kene
      An' strippit himsel o the scarlet red,
         An' put on the licht Lincoln Green, green, &c

3   Up it spak Johnnie's mither,
         An' a wae, wae woman was she.
      I beg you bide at hame Johnnie,
         I pray be ruled by me, me, &c

4   Baken bread ye sall nae lack,
         An' wine you sall lack nane,
      Oh! Johnnie for my benison
         I beg you bide at hame, hame, &c

5   He has made a solemn aith,
         Atween the sun an' the mune,
      That he wald gae to the gude greenwood,
         The dun deer to ding doon, doon, &c

6   He luiket east, he luiket wast,
         An' in below the sun,

75

And there he saw the dun deer –
Below a bush o' broom.

7   The first and shot that Johnnie shot
         He wounded her in the side –
     The next and shot that Johnnie shot
         I wat he laid her pride.

   8   He's eaten o' the venison – ,
         And drunken o' the bloud,
     Until he's fallen as sound asleep
         As though he had been dead.

   9   By there cam a silly auld man –
         And a silly auld man was he,
     For he's on to the seven foresters –
         As fast as he can flee.

   10 As I cam in along the haughs –
         And in among the scrogs,
     The bonniest boy that ere I saw
         Lay sleepin' atween his dogs.

          . . . .

   11 The first an shot that Johnnie shot
         He killed them a' but ane –
     And he flang him owre a milk white steed
         And bade him bear tidings hame.

76

An' there he spied the dun deer,
  Aneath a bush o' brume, brume, &c.

7   The firsten shot that Johnnie shot
      He wounded her in the Side.
    The nexten shot that Johnnie shot,
      I wat he laid her pride, pride, &c

8   He's eaten o the venison,
      An drunken o the blude
    Until he fell as sound asleep,
      As though he had been dead, dead
      As though he had been dead.

9   Bye there cam a silly Auld Man,   f. 25ᵛ
      And a silly auld man was he;
    An' he's on to the seven foresters,
      As fast as he can flee, flee, &c

10   "As I cam in by yonder haugh;
     "An' in among the scroggs
    "The bonniest boy that ere I saw,
     "Lay sleepin atween his dogs, dogs, &c

        . . . .

11   The firsten shot that Johnnie shot,
     He shot them a' but ane;
    An' he flang him owre a milkwhite steed,
     Bade him bear tidings, hame, hame, &c

Note. I have heard another version where Johnnie is slain, and thrown "owre a milk white steed". News is sent to Johnnies mother who flies to her son, but,

      Aye at ilka ae mile's end,
       She fand a *cut o clay –
      An' written upon the back o it,
       Tak your son Johnnie Brod away.

* bunch of straw daubed with clay, used for building cottages.

14

Burd Helen
[Child no. 258 Broughty Wa's]

p. 33

Burd He - len was her Moth- er's dear,—   Her Fa - ther's heir to   be;   He—

was   the Laird o'   Broch- ty Wa's, An'——   Pro - vost o'   Dun - dee.

1   Burd Helen was her mother dear
        Her father's heir to be –
     He was the Laird o' Broughty halls
        O' Broughty ne'ar Dundee.

2   Burd Helen she was much admired,
        By all that were round about.
     But to Hunglen she was betrothed
        Her virgin days were out.

3   Glen Hazlen was a comely youth,
        And virtuous his freinds,
     He left the schools o bonnie Dundee
        And he's on to Aberdeen.

4   It fell out once upon a time
        Burd Helen was left alone
     A' for to keep her father's tours
        They stand two miles from toun.

5   Glen Hazlen he cam ridin' by
        A' thinkin' to win in –

14

Burd Hellen, or Broughty Wa's   (Mrs Harris)
[Child no. 258 Broughty Wa's]

1   Burd Hellen was her mother's dear,
        Her father's hier to be.
     He was the Laird o' Brochty Walls,
        An' Provost of Dundee.

2   Burd Hellen she was much admired;
        By all that were round aboot,
     But to Hunglen she was betrothed,
        Her virgin days were out.

3   Glenhazlen was a comely youth,   f. 18^{r}
        An' virtuous his frien's
     He left the schules o' bonnie Dundee,
        An' on to Aberdeen.

4   It fell oot once upon a time,
        Burd Hellen was left alone,
     All for to keep her father's tours,
        They stand two miles from toun.

5   Glenhazlen he cam ridin' bye,
        An' thinkin to get in,

But the wind it blew and the rain dang on
And weet him to the skin.

6   He was very well entertained
       Baith for his bed and board
     Till a band o' men surrounded them
       Weel armed wi spear and sword.

7   They heysed her along with them,
       Locked up her maids behind –
p. 34   And flang the Keys out owre the wa's
       That none the plot might find.

8   They heysed her alang wi' them
       Owre mony a rock and glen
     And a' that he could say or do,
       To weep she would not refrain.

9   It fell out once upon a day
       They went out to take the air
     She threw hersel in to the stream,
       Against wind and despair –

10   It was sae deep he couldna wade
       Boats waurna to be found
     So he leapt in after her himsel,
       And he sank down like a stone

11   She kilted up her green cleadin'
       A little below her knee,
     And she never rest, nor was undrest,
       Till she reached again Dundee –

But the wind it blew, an' the rain dang on;
  An' wat him to the skin.

6   He was very weel entertained,
     Baith for his bed an' board;
    Till a band o' men, surrounded them,
     Well armed wi spear, & sword.

7   They hiesèd her along wi them,
     Locked up her maids behind,
    An' flang the keys outowre the wa's
     That none the plot might find.

8   They hiesèd her along wi them,
     Owre mony a rock an' glen;
    But a' that they could say or do;
     To weep she wald not refrain.

9   "The hieland hills are high, high hills,
     "The hieland hills are hie –
    "An' if you wald my favour gain,
     "Oh! tak me to Dundee."

10   It fell out once upon a time,
     They went oot to tak the air,
    She threw hersel in-to the stream,
     Between wind an' despair.

11   The stream was deep, he couldna wade,   f. 18ᵛ
     Boats waurna to be found,
    So he leapt in after her himsel,
     An' sank doun like a stone.

12   "The highland hills are high, high hills,
     The highland hills are hie.
     Their no like the pleasant banks o' the Tay,
     Nor the bonnie toun o' Dundee –

13   I learned this at broughty Was'
     At Broughty near Dundee
     That if Water were my prison strong –
     I could swim for Liberty."

15

p. 35   Charlie Macpherson
          [Child no. 234 Charlie MacPherson]

1   Charlie Macpherson that braw hieland lad
     On Valentine's ee'n gaed doun to Kinalty
     Courted Burd Helen, baith waukin' and sleepin
     Oh fair fa' them has my love in keepin'.

2   Charlie Macpherson cam doun the dykeside
     Baith Milton and Muirton and a' being his guide
     Baith Milton and Muirton, and auld Water Nairn
     A gaed wi' him for to be his warnin'

3   When he cam to the house o' Kinalty
     "Open your yetts Mistress and lat us come in
     Open your yetts Mistress, and lat us come in,
     For here's a commission come frae your gude son' –

12   "The highland hills are high, high hills,
        "The highland hills are hie,
      "They're no like the pleasant banks o' Tay,
        "Nor the bonnie toun o' Dundee."

13   She kilted up her green cleiden,
        A little below her knee,
      An' never rest, nor was undrest,
        Till she reached again Dundee.

14   "I learnt this at Brochty Walls,
        "At Brochty near Dundee,
      "That if water waur my prison walls
        "I could swim for liberty."

15

                    Charlie MacPherson   (Mrs Harris)
        [Child no. 234 Charlie MacPherson]
              Air "Whilk o' ye lasses"

1   Charlie Macpherson that braw hieland lad,   f. 23ᵛ
     On Valentine's even cam doun to Kinaltie,   no. 21
     Courtit Burd Hellen, baith wakin' an' sleepin,
     Oh! fair fa' them, has my love in keepin.

2   Charlie Macpherson cam doun the dykeside,
     Baith Milton, an' Muirton an' a' bein his guide,
     Baith Milton an' Muirton an' auld Water Nairn,
     A' gaed wi him for to be his warn.

3   Whan he cam to the hoose o' Kinaltie
     Open your yetts, Mistress, an' lat us come in;
     "Open your yetts Mistress an' lat us come in
      "For here's a commission, come frae your
                                        [gudeson.

83

4   Madam" says Charlie "Whaur's your dochter
      Mony a time have I come to Kinalty and sought her
      Now mast she go wi' me many a mile
      Because I've brought mony a man frae the West
                                    [Isle."

5   'As for my dochter she has gone abroad,
      You'll no get her for her tocher gude –
      She's on to Whitehouse to marry the —
      Oh fair fa' them that wait on my bairn' –

6   Charlie Macpherson gaed up the dykeside
      Baith Milton and Muirton and a' being his guide
      Baith Milton, and Muirton, and Auld Water Nairn
      A' gaed wi' him for to be his warnin'.

7   When they cam to the house o' Brae Mar,
      So weel as he kent that his Nelly was there –
      And Nelly was sittin' upon her bedside
      And every one there was callin' her, "Bride"

p. 36

8   The Candles gaed out, they were na weel lichted
      Swords and spears they glancèd fu' bricht.
      So laith as she was her true love to beguile,
      Because he brocht mony a man frae the West Isle.

4   "Madam," says Charlie, whare s your dochter –
     "Mony time have I come to Kinatie an' socht her,
     "Noo maun she goe wi me mony a mile –
     "Because I've brocht mony men frae the west
                                              [Isle."

5   'As for my dochter she has gane abroad,
     'You'll no get her for her tocher gude –
     'She's on to Whitehouse, to marry auld Gairn,
     'Oh! fair fa' them that wait on my bairn.'

6   Charlie MacPherson gaed up the dykeside,
     Baith Muirtoun an' Milton an' a' bein' his guide –
     Baith Muirton an' Milton, an' Auld Water Nairn –
     A' gaed wi him for to be his warn.

7   Whan he cam to the hoose in Braemar,
     Sae weel as he kent that his Nellie was there.
     An' Nellie was sittin upon the bed side,
     An' every one there was ca'ing her, *bride*.

8   The can'les gaed oot, they waurna weel licht,
     Swords an' spears they glancit fou bricht –
     Sae laith as she was her true love to beguile,
     Because he brocht mony men frae the West Isle –

16

Mary Hamilton
[Child no. 173 Mary Hamilton]

1   My Mother was a proud, proud woman,
        A Proud woman, and a bold,
      And she sent me to Queen Mary s bours,
        When scarcely eleven years old –

2   Queen Mary's bread it was sae sweet –
        And her wine it was sae fine –
      That
        And I rued it aye sene syne.

3   Queen Mary she cam doun the stair,
        Wi the gowd kaim in her hair –
      "Oh where, oh where is the wee wee babe
        I heard greitin sae sair.?"

4   'Its no a babe a baby fair,
        Nor ever intends to be,
      But I myself wi a sair colic –
        Was sick and like to dee.'

16

Marie Hamilton   (Mrs Harris
[*Child no. 173 Mary Hamilton*]   & others)

f. 40^r
no. 9

1   My mother was a proud, proud woman,   f. 10^v
           A proud woman, and a bold;   no. 6
       She sent me to Queen Marie's bour;
           When scarcely eleven years old.

2   Queen Marie's bread, it was sae sweet,
           An' her wine, it was sae fine;
       That I hae lien in a young man's arms,
           An' I rued it aye synsyne.

3   Queen Marie she cam doon the stair,   f. 11^r
           Wi the goud kaims in her hair;
       "Oh! whare, oh whare, is the wee wee babe,
           I heard greetin sae sair?"

4   'Its no a babe, a babie fair,
           'Nor ever intends to be,
       'But I mysel wi a sair colic,
           'Was sick an' like to dee.'

87

5   They sought the bed baith up and doun,
       Frae the pillow to the straw,
    And there they got the wee, wee babe
       But the life was far awa.

p. 37   6   "Go dress, go dress Mary Hamilton
       Go dress and make you fine –

. . . .

7   You'll no put on your dowie black,
       Nor yet your dowie broun –
    But you'll put on your red, red silks
       To shine through Edinburgh town."

. . . .

8   'Yestreen the Queen had four Maries,
       The nicht she'll hae but three
    There was Mary Seton, and Mary Bethune
       And Mary Carmichael and me.

9   Oh little did my mither ken
       On the day she cradled me
    The lands that I should travel in
       And the death that I should dee.'

10   There was Mary Seton, & Mary Behune,
       And Mary Carmichael and me."
    But the bonniest Mary among them a'
       Was hanged upon a tree.

5   They socht the bed, baith up an' doon;
        Frae the pillow to the straw,
    An there they got the wee wee babe;
        But its life was far awa'.

6   "Come doon, come doon Marie Hamilton,
        "Come doon an speak to me.

            . . . .

7   "You'll no put on your dowie black,
        "Nor yet your dowie broun,
        "But you'll put on your ried, ried silk
        "To shine through Edinborough toun."

            . . . .

8   'Yestreen the Queen had four Marie's,
        'The nicht she'll hae but three,
        'There was Marie Bethune, an' Marie Seaton,
        'An' Marie Carmichael an' me.

9   'Ah little did my mither ken,
        'The day she cradled me;
        'The lands that I sud travel in,
        'An' the death that I suld dee.'

10   Yestreen the Queen had four Marie's
        The nicht she has but three –
    For the bonniest Marie amang them a'
        Was hanged upon a tree.

17

Sweet William
[Child no. 106 The Famous Flower of Serving-Men]

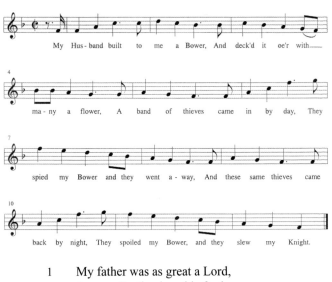

My Hus-band built to me a Bower, And deck'd it oe'r with—— ma-ny a flower, A band of thieves came in by day, They spied my Bower and they went a-way, And these same thieves came back by night, They spoiled my Bower, and they slew my Knight.

1   My father was as great a Lord,
     As ever Scotland could aford
     My mother was a Lady bright,
     My husband was a gallant knight –

2   My husband built to me a bowr
     And decked it oer with many a flower
     A band of theives cam in by day
     They spied my bowr and they went away.
p. 38   And these same thieves cam back by night
     They spied my bower and they slew my knight

3   Now after that my love was slain,
     And I could no longer there remain,
     My servants all from me did flee –
     In the midst of my extremitie.

17

Sweet William   (Mrs Harris)

[Child no. 106 The Famous Flower of Serving-Men]

f. 43^r

no. 24

1   My husband built for me a bower,   f. 20^r
     An' decked it oe'r with many a flowr,   no. 15
     A band of theives cam in by day –
     They spied my bowr and they went away,
     And these same thieves cam back by night –
     They spied my bowr, and they slew my knight.

2   Then after that my knight was slain,
     I could no longer there remain –
     My servants all from me did flee –
     In the midst of my extremetie.

4   With a double ruff, and a beaver hat
          And a golden band about my neck –
          With a silver rapier by my side –
          So like a gallant I did ride.

. . . .

5   "Oh will you be one of my guard?
          And you will get a great reward –
          Or will you be taster o' my wine?
          To wait upon me when I do dine.

6   Or will you be waiter of my hall?
          To wait upon my nobles all
          Or will you be my Chamberlain?
          To make my bed both soft & fine,"

7   I winna be one of your guard,
          Tho' I should get a great reward
          Nor will I be taster o' your wine
          To wait upon you when you do dine –

8   I will not be waiter o' your hall
          To wait upon your nobles all
          But I will be your chamberlain,
          To make your bed both soft and fine.'

p. 39   9   One day the King did a hunting go –

. . . .

10   "My father was as great a Lord,
          As ever Scotland could aford –
          My mother was a Lady bright –
          My husband was a gallant knight.

11   My husband built for me a bower
          And deckt it oe'r with many a flower –
          A band of thieves cam in by day –
          They spied my bowr and they went away.

3   'With a double ruff, and a beaver hat,   f. 20^v
     'And a golden band about my neck –
     'A silver rapier by my side,
     'So like a gallant, I did ride.

. . . .

4   'Oh will you be one o' my guards –
     'And I will give you a great reward,
     'Or will you be taster of my wine,
     'To wait upon me when I do dine,

5   'Or will you be master of my hall,
     'To wait upon my nobles all,
     'Or will you be my chamberlain,
     'To make my bed, both soft an' fine.

6   "I wilna be one o' your guard,
     "Though you should give me a great reward.
     "I winna be taster o' your wine,
     "To wait upon you when you do dine.

7   "I winna be master o' your hall,
     "To wait upon your nobles all,
     "But I will be your chamberlain,
     "To make your bed baith saft an' fine."

8   One day the king did a hunting go,

. . . .

9   "My Husband built for me a bowr,
     "And decked it oe'r wi many a flower.
     "A band of thieves cam in by day
     "They spied my bower, and they went away,

And these same thieves cam back by nigh[t]
They spied my bowr and they slew my knigh[t]

12   Now after that my knight was slain
      And I could no longer there remain –
      My servants all from me did flee
      In the midst of my extremetie. "

. . . .

13   'What news, what news," the King did sa[y]
      "None but Sweet William is a lady gay'

. . . .

14   Was ever the like heard or seen
      Of a gentleman to become a queen –

"And these same thieves came back by night.
"They spied my bower and they slew my knight.

10   "After that my knight was slain,
      "I could no langer there remain.
      "My servants all from me did flee,
      "I the midst of my extremetie.

11   With a double ruff, and a beaver hat,   f. 21ʳ
      And a golden band about my neck.
      A silver rapier by my side –
      So like a gallant I did ride.

. . . .

12   'What news, what news,' the king did say,
      'None, but William is a lady gay."

. . . .

13   Was ever the like heard or seen –
      For a gentleman, to become a queen.'

18

Fair Margaret
[Child no. 63 Child Waters]

1   "I beg you bide at hame Margaret
And sew your silken seam –
For if you were in the wide hielands
You wad be owre far frae hame."

p. 40   2   'I winna bide at hame,' she said
Nor sew my silken seam –
For If I were in the wide hielands,
I wad no be owre far frae hame.'

3   "My hounds shall eat the bread o' wheat,
And you the bread o' bran' –
I'll mak you sigh and say, alas!
That ever I lo'ed a man"

18

Fair Margaret   (Mrs Harris)
[Child no. 63 Child Waters]

f. 40^r
no. 7

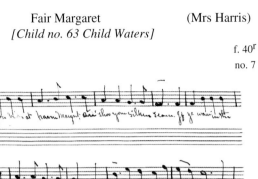
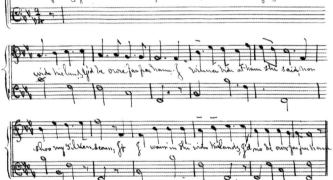

1   "I beg you bide at hame Margaret,   f. 12^v
     An' sew your silken seam.   no. 8
     If ye waur in the wide Hielands
     Ye wald be owre far frae hame."

2   "I winna bide at hame," she said,   f. 13^r
     "Nor sew my silken seam;
     'For if I waur in the wide hielands
     'I wald no be owre far frae hame.'

4   'Tho' your hounds do eat the bread o' wheat
    And me, the bread o' bran –
Yet will I sing and merry be;
    That ever I lo'ed a man' –

5   "My steed shall drink the blude red wine
    And you the water wan –
I'll mak you sigh and say, alas!
    That ever I loed Lord John – "

6   'Tho' your steed does drink the blude red wine
    And me the water wan,
Yet will I sing and merry be,
    That ever I lo'ed Lord John.'

7   He turned aboot his high horse head
    And away he was bound to ride –
She kilted up her green cleading
    And after him she gaed.

8   When they cam to that water
    That a' man ca' the Clyde,
He turned aboot his high horse head,
    Says, "Lady will you ride."

p. 41   9   'I learned it in my mother's bour
    I wish I hae learned it weel;
That I can swim this wan water,
    As weel as fish or eel – '

3   "My steed sall drink the blude red wine,
         "An' you the water wan;
     "I'll mak you sigh, an' say alace!
         That ever I loed a man."

4   'Though your steed does drink the blude red wine,
         'An' me the water wan,
     'Yet will I sing an' merry be
         'That ever I loed a man.'

5   "My hounds shall eat the bread o' wheat,
         "An' you the bread o' bran,
     "Ill mak you sigh an' say alace!
         "That ever you loed Lord John."

6   "Though your hounds do eat the bread o' wheat,
         'An' me the bread o' bran
     'Yet will I sing an' merrie be
         'That ever I loed Lord John.

7   He turned aboot his high horse head,
         An' awa he was boun to ride.
     She kilted up her green clieden,
         An' after him she gaed.

8   Whan they cam to that water,
         Whilk a' man ca' the Clyde,
     He turned aboot his high horse head,
         Said, "Ladie will you ride?"

9   'I learnt it in my mother's bour,   f. 13ᵛ
         'I wish I had learnt it weel – '
     'That I culd swim this wan water,
         'As weel as fish or eel.'

10   Whan at the middle o' that water,
         She sat doon on a stone,
     He turned aboot his high horse head,
         Says, "Ladie will ye loup on?"

10   He has taen the narrow ford
      And she has taen the wide –
    Lang, lang e'er he was at the middle o' tha[t]
      She was sittin at the other side

11   Aye at the middle o' that water
      I'm sure there is a stone
    He turned aboot his high horse head
      Says, "Lady will you loup on?"

12   'I learned it in my mother's bour –
      I wish I had learned it better,
    That I can swim this wan water
      As weel as eel or otter – '

13   When she cam to the other side,
      She sat down on a stone.
    Wi' sighin said that fair Margaret
      'Alas! I'm far frae home.

14   How mony miles is't to your castle,
      Now Lord John tell to me – '
    "How mony miles is't to my castle?
      Its thirty miles and three."
    Wi' sighin said that Fair Margaret,
      'It will never be gaen by me.'

p. 42   15   But up it spak the wily bird,
      As it sat on the tree.
    "Rin on, rin on, you Fair Margaret
      It scarcely is miles three – "

11   'I learnt it in my mothers bour,'
'I wish I had learnt it better,'
'That I culd swim this wan water,
'As well as eel or otter.'

12   He has taen the narrow ford,
An' she has taen the wide
Lang, lang ere he was at the middle,
She was sittin at the ither side.

. . . .

13   Wi sighen said that Fair Margaret,
'Alace! I'm far frae home.'

14   "Hoo mony miles is't to your Castle?
Noo Lord John tell to me."
'Hoo mony miles is't to my Castle?
'It's thirty miles an three.'
Wi' sighen said that Fair Margaret,
"It'll never be gane by me."

15   But up it spak the wily bird,
As it sat on the tree.
'Rin on, rin on, noo Fair Margaret
'It scarcely miles, is three.'

16 When they cam to the wide hielands
   And lichted on the green,
  Every ane spak Erse to anither
   But Margaret she spak nane.

17 There was mony a knicht, and Lady bricht
   Led Lord John to the ha',
  But the best blude among them a',
   Led his steed to the sta' –

18 There was mony a knicht, and Lady bricht
   Led Lord John to the Table
  But the gentlest blude among them a'
   Led his steed to the stable –

19 There was mony a kicht, and Lady bricht
   Led Lord John to the room,
  But the gentlest blude amang them a'
   Was Lord John's stable groom –

20 When they were at table set,
   And birlin at the best
  Margaret sat at a bye table;
   And fain she wad haen rest.

21 "Oh! mother, mother make my bed,
   Wi clean blankets and sheets;
  And Lay my foot boy at my feet
   The sounder I may sleep."

p. 43 22 She has made Lord John his bed
   Wi clean blankets and sheets,
  And laid his foot boy at his feet
   The sounder he might sleep.

23 'Win up, win up nou Fair Margaret,
   And see that my steed has meat
  See that his corn is in his travise
   Or Lying amang his feet."

16   Whan they cam to the wide Hielands,   f. 14^r
        An' lichted on the green;
      Every an' spak Ershe to anither
        But Margaret, she spak nane.

17   Whan they waur at table set,
        An' birlin at the best,
      Margaret set at a bye table;
        An' fain she wald hain rest.

18   "Oh! Mither, mither, mak my bed,
        Wi clean blankets an' sheets;
      An' lay my futeboy at my feet,
        The sounder I may sleep."

19   She has made Lord John his bed;
        Wi clean blankets an' sheets,
      An' laid his futeboy at his feet,
        But ne'er a wink culd he sleep.

20   "Win up, win up noo Fair Margaret,
        "An' see that my steed has meat.
      "See that his corn is in his travis.
        "Or lyin amang his feet."

24   Slowly, slowly rase she up –
        And slowly put she on;
     And slowly went she doun the stair,

. . . .

25   'An askin, an askin Gude Lord John,
        I pray you grant it me
     That the warst bed in a' your house
        That you may gie to me – '

26   "Your askin is but sma Margaret
        Sune granted it sall be
     For the best bed in a' my house
        Is ower little for thee – "

27   'An askin, an askin gude Lord John,
        I pray you grant it me,
     That the warst ale in a' your house,
        That you may gie to me'

28   Your askin is but sma' Margaret,
        Sune granted it sall be
     For the best wine in a' my house –
        Is ower little for thee –

p. 44   29   "But cheer up your heart, nou Fair Margaret
        For be it as it may.
     Your Kirkin' and your Fair weddin'
        Sall baith be on one day."

21   Slowly, slowly rase she up,
      An' slowly put she on,
    An' slowly gaed she doon the stair,
      Aye makin a heavy moan.

. . . .

22   'An asken, an asken gude Lord John –
      'I pray you grant it me.
    'For the warst bed in a' your hoose,
      'To your young son an' me."

23   "Your asken is but sma Margaret,   f. 14$^\mathrm{v}$
      "Sune grantet it sall be –
    "For the best bed in a' my hoose,
      "Is owre little for thee"

24   'An' asken, an asken gude Lord John,
      'I pray you grant it me;
    'For the warst ale in a your hoose –
      'That ye wald gie to me.'

25   "Your asken is but sma' Margaret,
      "Sune grantet it sall be,
    "For the best wine in a my hoose,
      "Is owre little for thee.

26   "But cheer up your heart noo Fair Margaret
      "For be it as it may
    "Your kirken, an' your fair weddin,
      'Sall baith be on one day."

19

Andrew Cowper

1 "Its lang, Lang to Lammas,
  Till I see my dear,
 I long to be with her
  When the evenings are clear

2 When the evenings are clear
  And the dew fallin' doun
 I long to be with her
  By the light o' the moon – "

    . . . .

3 There's gold in my coffers
  But there's nane in Lochblair."

19

Andrew Coupar   (Mrs Harris)

f. 42^v
no. 22

1   Its lang, lang to Lammas,   f. 23^r
        "Till I see my dear   no. 20
     "I long to be with her
        "When the evenings are clear.

2   "When the evenings are clear,
        "An' the dew fallin doon
     "I long to be with her,
        "By the light o' the moon."

4   "Ah! waes me Cluny
      Wi your ha's and your towers
    You've wedded my Jeanie
      Wi your orchards' o' flowers."

5   Ah! waes me Cluny
      Wi your orchards o' thyme –
    You ve wedded my Jeannie
      Wha should have been mine – "

. . . .

6   Bonnie Andrew Cowper
      His sword out he drew
    And he swore that through Cluny
      He would mak it go through –

p. 45   7   Haud your hand Andrew Cowper
      You'll ne'er kill a man – '
    Ere he had the words spoken
      He made him lie slain

. . . .

Note.

    Jeanie's daughter by Cluny married into the Airlie family, and brought with her the estate of Cluny. Her portrait is among the family pictures at Cortachy Castle.

3   "Ah! waes me Cluny,
      "Wi your orchards o' thyme
     You've wedded my Jeannie
      "That s'ud hae been mine.

4   "Ah! waes me Cluny,
      "Wi your ha's an' your tours,
     "You've wedded my Jeanie,
      "Wi your orchards an' flowers."

            . . . .

5   'Theres gowd in my coffers,
     But there's nane in Lochblair.'

6   Bonnie Andrew Coupar,
      His sword out he drew,
     An' he swore that through Cluny
      He wald make it go through.

7   'Haud your hand, Andrew Coupar,
      'You'll neer kill a man,'
     Ere he had the word spoken,
      He made him lie slain.

The fragment of "Andrew Coupar" is connected with the
Airlie family, by a   tragical affair took place more than a   f. 2ᵛ
century ago, in the churchyard of Caputh, in Perthshire. Andrew
Coupar, Laird of Lochblair, (a small property now merged among
others in the Estate of Rosemount, near Blairgowrie) loved and
was affianced to Jeanie Ogilvy, cousin to Ogilvy the Daft Laird of
Cluny Castle, between Blairgowrie and Dunkeld. Jeanie's
affections were centred on Lochblair, but her parents' entreaties
and her own fear of offending her powerful and violent relative
induced her to break her engagement, and become his wife. The
two rivals met at a funeral in the churchyard of Caputh. Cowpar
laid his hand on his sword, gave Cluny a pretty broad taunt, who
raised his pistol, and shot him dead on the spot. After exclaiming

19 Andrew Cowper

"You miss, I kiss." he immediately fled to France, where he remained till Coupar's sisters agreed to accept a sum of money and sist proceedings against him. They afterwards resided at Newton Castle, shunned by all, on account of selling their brother's blood. Cluny returned home and resided with his wife, at Cluny Castle, which is situated on an island near the margin of the Loch – the lady led a miserable life by reason of her husband's mad freaks. On one occasion he conveyed a wild colt accross, and drove it into the appartment in which she sat. In her terror she took shelter in the chimney, and remained there until her f. 3ʳ Lord thought proper to relieve her of her dangerous companion. On another occasion he set her adrift in an open boat, which had previously been pierced with holes. In order to keep the boat afloat, she was obliged to stop the holes with shreds of her clothes. Their only child and hieress, was married, and brought the estate of Cluny, into the Airlie family; and her portrait is shown among the ancestral pictures at Cortachy Castle.

There are still lingering reminiscences of Cluny in the districts of Blairgowrie and Alyth – near which latter place he lies buried, by his own desire, beside his horse and dog. The spot is near the public road, enclosed by a stone wall. The Laird's pistol seems to have been his constant attendant. When he wanted his ploughman from the field, his plan was to aim at the ploughshare. When he wanted amusement, to order his servant to stand at a certain distance with a piece of slate in his hand for a target. The said serving man after his master's death, exercised the profession of Whittlegait Dominie in the district of Manse, in the parish of Blairgowrie. His name was James Ritchie, and the last of his infantile pupils, the late Venerable Father of the Church of Scotland, died in 1867 aged 93.

20

The Kitchen Boy
[Child no. 252 The Kitchie-Boy]

1   There lived a lady in the North
      Of muckle birth and fame,
    She fell in love wi her Kitchen Boy
      And the greater was her shame.

2   She called on her kitchen boy

          . . . .

3   "For Master Cook he will cry out,
      And answered he maun be."

4   'I hae a coffer o' red gowd
      My mother left to me
    And I will build a bonnie ship
      And send it to the sea –

          . . . .

5   And you'll come hame like lord or squire
      And answered you maun be.'

6   She has built a bonnie ship,
      And sent it ower the main;
    And in a towmont or thereby
      The ship cam back again.

7   Gae dress, gae dress my dochter Janet,
      Gae dress and make you fine –
    And you'll gae down to yon shore side,
      And bid yon lords to dine.'

          . . . .

20

The Kitchie Boy   (Mrs Harris
[Child no. 252 The Kitchie-Boy]   & others)

1   There lived a Lady in the north,   f. 21$^\mathrm{r}$
      O' muckle birth an' fame,   no. 16
    She's faun in love wi her kitchie boy,
      The greater was her shame.

          . . . .

2   "Maister Cook, he will cry oot,
      "An' answered he maun be."

3   I hae a coffer o' ried gowd,
      My mither left to me,
    An' I will build a bonnie ship,
      And send her ower the sea,
    An' you'll come hame like Lord or Squire,
      An' answered you maun be.

4   She has biggit a bonnie ship –
      Sent her across the main,
    An' in less than sax months an' a day,
      That ship cam back again.

5   'Go dress, go dress, my dochter Janet,
      'Go dress an' mak you fine,
    'An' we'll go doun to yon shore side,
      'An' bid yon lords to dine.'

p. 46   8   He pued a black mask ower his face,
                       Kaimed down his yellow hair;
                    And a' for fear it should be kenned
                       That ever he had been there.

                       . . . .

            9   "Oh got you that by sea sailin'.
                       Or got you that by land?
                    Or got you that on Spanish coast,
                       Upon a dead man's hand?"

           10   'I got na that by sea sailin'
                       I got na that by land
                    But I got that on Spanish coast,
                       Upon a dead man's hand.'

                       . . . .

           11   He pued the black mask off his face
                       Flang back his yellow hair,

                       . . . .

           12   "A priest, a priest" the Lady cryed
                       To marry my love and me – "
                    A clerk, a clerk, her father cryed
                       To sign, her tocher free.

6   He's pued the black mask ower his face,   f. 21^V
         Kaimed doun his yellow hair –
     A' no to lat her father ken,
         That ere he had been there.

                    . . . .

7   'Oh! got you that by sea sailin
         'Or got you that by land,
     'Or got you that on Spanish coast,
         'Upon a died man's hand?

8   "I got na that by sea sailin
         "I got na that by land,
     "But I got that on Spanish coast,
         "Upon a deid man's hand."

                    . . . .

9   He's pued the black mask aff his face,
     Threw back his yellow hair.

                    . . . .

10   "A priest, a priest," the lady she cried
         "To marry my love, an' me."
     'A clerk, a clerk," her father cried
         To sign her tocher free.'

21

Robin
              [Child no. 277 The Wife Wrapt in Wether's Skin]

1   Robin he's gane to the Wast,
          Hollin green hollin –
       He's waled a wife among the warst
          Bend your bows Robin.

2   She could niether wash nor wring –
          Hollin green hollin –
       For spoilin' o' her gay gold ring.
          Bend your bows Robin.

3   She could niether bake nor brew;
          Hollin green hollin.
       For spoilin' o' her bonnie hue.
          Bend your bows Robin.

4   She could niether spin nor caird,
          Hollin green hollin –
       But fill the cup and sair the Laird.
          Bend your bows Robin.

5   Robin's sworn by the rude –
          Hollin green hollin –
       That he wad mak an ill wife gude.
          Bend your bows Robin.

6   Robin he's gane to the fauld.
          Hollin green hollin.
       And tane his black sheep by the spauld –
          Bend your bows Robin.

21

Robin he's gane to the wude   (Mrs Harris)
[Child no. 277 The Wife Wrapt in Wether's Skin]
Air "Jo Janet"

1   Robin he's gane to the wast,   f. 26^v
        Hollin green hollin.   no. 25
      He's waled a wife amang the warst.
        Bend your bows Robin

2   She could niether bake, nor brew.
        Hollin green hollin,
      For spoilin o' her bonnie hue,
        Bend your bows Robin.

3   She could niether spin nor caird,
        Hollin green hollin –
      But fill the cup an' sair the Laird
        Bend your bows Robin.

4   She could niether wash nor wring –   f. 27^r
        Holin green holin.
      For spoilin o' her gay goud ring,
        Bend your bows Robin.

5   Robin's sworn by the rude,
        Hollin green hollin.
      That he wald mak an ill wife gude.
        Bend your bows Robin.

6   Robin he's gane to the fauld,
        Hollin green hollin.
      An' taen his black [sheep] by the spauld –
        Bend your bow Robin.

117

p. 52   7   He's tane aff his wether's skin,
              Hollin green hollin –
          And he has prinned his ain wife in.
              Bend your bows Robin.

      8   "I daurna beat my wife for a' her kin,
              Hollin green hollin
          But I can beat my wethers skin.
              Bend your bows Robin."

      9   'I can baith bake and brew,
              Hollin green hollin.
          What care I for my bonnie hue.
              Bend your bows Robin.

      10   I can baith wash and wring,
              Hollin green hollin –
          What care I for my gay gold ring –
              Bend your bows Robin.

      11   I can baith spin and caird,
              Hollin green hollin.
          Lat ony body sair the Laird,
              Bend your bows Robin.'

      12   Robin he's gane to the wode
              Hollin green hollin.
          And there he made an ill wife gude
              Bend your bows Robin.

7   He's taen aff his withers skin,
       Hollin green hollin,
     An' he has preened his ain wife in,
       Bend your bows Robin.

8   I daurna beat my wife for a' her kin.
       Hollin green hollin.
     But I may beat my withers skin.
       Bend your bows Robin.

9   'I can baith bake an' brew,
       Hollin green hollin.
     'What care I for my bonnie hue,'
       Bend your bows Robin.

10   'I can baith wash an wring,
      'Hollin green hollin
    'What care I for my gay gowd ring.'
      'Bend your bows Robin.

11   'I can baith spin an' caird,
      'Hollin green hollin.
    'Lat ony bodie sair the Laird.
      'Bend your bow Robin.

12   Robin's sworn by the rude,
      Hollin green hollin,
    That he has made an ill wife gude,
      Bend your bow Robin.

22

Teedle ell O

1   Robin made his testament.
             Upon a coll o' hay.
         And by cam the greedy gled –
           Stole Robin quite away –
               Teedle ell O, teedle ell O,
                 Sing toora reedle ell
               Sing fara roodle little oodle
                 Toora Reedle ell.

2   Ye'll tak aff my bonnie head,
             It is baith round and sma' –
         And gied to the herds o Hamilton –
           To play at the fit ba!
               Teedle ell O, &c

3   Ye'll tak aff my bonnie neb –
             Tha pickles out the corn.
         And gied to the herds o' Hamilton
           To be a tootin horn.
               Teedle ell O – &c

4   Ye'll tak aff my bonnie legs –
             That are baith sma and trig,
         And gie them to the toon o' Hamilton
           To be pillars to the brig.
               Teedle ell O. &c

22

Robin's Tes'ment   (Mrs Harris)

1   Robin's made his tes'ment,   f. 32ʳ
     Upon a' cole o' hay,   no. 38
     An' by cam the greedy gled;
     Stole Robin quite away –
         Teedle ell o, teedle ello
         Toora reedle ell –
         Sing far-a roodle, little oodle
         Toora reedle ell.

2   You'll tak aff my bonnie nib –
     That pickles oot the corn –
     An' gie't to the herds o' Hamilton,
     To be a toutin horn.
         Teedle ello – &c

3   You'll tak aff my bonnie head,
     It is baith round an' sma',
     An' gie't to the herds o' Hamilton –
     To play at the fute ba'.
         Teedle ell o – &c

4   You'll tak aff my bonnie legs,
     They are baith Lang an trig –
     Gie them to the toon o Hamilton;
     For pillars to the brig.
         Teedle ell O – &c

121

. . . .

23

Wearies Wells
[Child no. 4 Lady Isabel and the Elf-Knight]

. . . .

1   Monie a time have I and my brown foal
         Rode the water o' Wearie Wells.

2   He rode in, and she wade in,
         Till it took her to the knie –
      Wi sighin' said that fair Lady,
      "This wadin's no for me."

3   He rode in, and she wade in,
         Till it took her to the chin,
      Wi sighin said that fair Lady
      "I'll wade nae farer in."

5   You'll tak oot my bonnie tongue,
       That whistled loud an' shrill,
       An' gie't to the Kirk o' Hamilton,
        For clapper to the bell.
         Teedle el O – &c –

23

        Wearie's Wells   (Mrs Harris)
   [Child no. 4 Lady Isabel and the Elf-Knight]

      · · · · · · · · · ·

1   Mony a time I rade wi my broun foal,   f. 22ᵛ
      The Water o' Wearie's Wells.   no. 19

2   Leave aff, Leave aff your gey mantle,
      Its a gowd but the hem –
      Leave aff leave [aff] its far owre gude,
       To weet i' the saut see faem.

3   She wade in, an' he rade in,
      Till it took her to the knee.
      Wi sighin said that lady gay,
      "Sic wadin s no for me."

      · · · · · · · · · ·

3   He rode in, and she wade in,
      Till it took her to the chin,
      Wi sighin said that fair Lady
      "I'll wade nae farer in.

4   'Tak aff, tak aff that gay mantle –
       Its a' gowd but the hem –
       It ill befits that gay cleidin'
       To float upon the stream.'

. . . .

5   'Seven kings dochters I hae drowned,
       And the eight ane you shall be,'

. . . .

6   Lie you there, you fause young man,
       Where you thought to Lay me –

. . . .

24

Hughie Graham
[Child no. 191 Hughie Grame]

1   Dukes and Lords a huntin' gone
       Over hills and vallies clear.
       There the've bound him Hughie Graham
       For stealin' o' the Bishop's mare.

. . . .

5   "Sax kings dochters I hae drowned
       'An' the seventh you sall be.'

                . . . .

6   "Lie you there you fause young man
       "Where you thought to lay me.

                . . . .

24

                      Hughie Grame
              [Child no. 191 Hughie Grame]

1   Dukes an lords a huntin gane,   f. 27ᵛ
          Over hills an' vallies clear,   no. 27
       There the've bound him Hughie Grame
          For stealin o the Bishop's mare.

                . . . .

25

Brown Edom
[Child no. 98 Brown Adam]

His stu-die was o' the bea - ten goud; His ham-mer o' the pith, The

cords war o' the gude green silk, He blew his bel - lows with.

p. 49   . . . .

1   His studie was o' the beaten gowd,
      His hammer o' the pith –
    And the cords were o' the gude green silk
      He blew his bellows with.

2   It fell out once, upon a nicht,
      Brown Edom he thocht Lang –
    That he wad go to see his love,
      By the lee licht o' the mune.

. . . .

25

Broun Edom   (Mrs Harris)
[Child no. 98 Brown Adam]

f. 40^V
no. 10

. . . .   f. 27^V
no. 26

1   For wha ere had a lealer luve,
        Than Broun Edom the Smith.

2   His studie was o' the beaten gowd –
        His hammer o' the pith,
    His cords waur o' the gude green silk,
        That blew his bellows with.

3   It fell out ance upon a time,
        Broun Edom he thoucht lang;
    That he wald gae to see his luve,
        By the le licht o' the mune.

127

26

The Lady o' Arngosk
[Child no. 225 Rob Roy]

1   Rob has frae the hielands come,
      And to the Lawland border,
      And a' to court a bonnie Lass –
      To haud his house in order.

. . . .

2   And they hae brocht her to a bed
      And there they laid her down
      And they've taen aff her peticoat –
      And stript her o' her goun –

. . . .

27

The higher that the mountain is   (David Harris)

1   The higher that the mountain is,
      The lower grows the grass,
      The bonnier that the Lassie is –
      She needs the tocher less.

2   The aulder that the crab tree grows
      The sourer grow the plums,
      And the Langer that the cobler warks
      The harder grow his thumbs.

. . . .

26

An' they hae brocht her to a bed   (Mrs Isdale
    [Child no. 225 Rob Roy]   Dron)

1   An' they hae brocht her to a bed,   f. 27ᵛ
    An' they hae laid her doun –   no. 29
    An' they've ta'en aff her petticoat;
    An' stript her o' her o' her goun – *

    * verse of a ballad on Robin Oigg's elopement

28

p. 50   Hech hiegh Durham   (David Harris)

1   Hech hiegh Durham.
     Durham its a dainty lee –
   I saw the gallantest ram –
     That ever mine eyes did see –

2   The horns that were on his head,
     Wad have held an army o' men –
   The tongue that was in his head,
     Wad have filled them every one.

3   Ilka tooth that was in his head,
     Wad have held a lippie o' corn,
   And ae little toothie beside,
     Wad have made a tootin horn.

4   The woo that was on his back
     Wad have made fifty packs o' claith.
   And for to mak you lee –
     I'm sure I wad be laith.

. . . .

29

East Muir King
[Child no. 89 Fause Foodrage]

East muir King, an' Wast muir King, An' King o' Luve a' three. Its

they cuist ke - vils them a - mang. A - boot a gay la - die.

1   East muir King, & West muir King
       And King o' Luve all three,
    And they coost kevils them among –
       Aboot a fair Lady

2   East muir king he won the gold
       And Wast muir king the fee –
    But king o' Luve, wi his Lands sae broad
       Has won the fair Lady.

. . . .

29

East Muir King   (Mrs Harris, a
[Child no. 89 Fause Foodrage]   mere fragment of
                                   Jannie Scott's
                                   version)

f. 39^v

no. 6

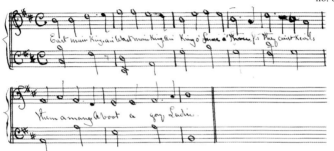

1   East muir king and wast muir king;   f. 22^r
        An' king o' Luve a' thrie,   no. 18
     Its they coost kevils, them amang,
        Aboot a gey ladie.

2   East Muir king, he wan the gowd,
        An' Wast Muir king the fee,
     But king a Luve, wi his lands sae broad,
        He's won the fair ladie.

3   Thae twa kings, they made an aith
        That be it as it may,
     They wad slay him king o' luve,
        Upon his waddin day.

4   East muir king, he brak his aith,   f. 22^v
        An sair penance did he.
     But Wast muir king, he made it oot,
        An' an ill deid may* he dee.   * or *mat*

. . . .

133

PART 2

SONGS APPEARING ONLY IN MS B

30

Earl of Aboyne   (Mrs Harris)
[Child no. 235 The Earl of Aboyne]

f. 41ᵛ
no. 16

Ye min - strels—— all, be at—— my—— call, Haud

a' your rooms a—— ring - in':   You may weel ken by her hair,

Wi' the dia - monds sae rare, That the Earl o' A - boyne—— is—— co - min

1   My Maidens fair, yoursels prepare,   f. 21ᵛ
no. 17

. . . .

2   You may weel knaw by her hair,
        Wi' the diamonds sae rare –
          That the Earl of Aboyne was comin.

3   My Minstrels all, be at my call,
       Haud a your rooms aringin,
       . . . .
f. 22^r   For the Earl of Aboyne is comin.

                . . . .

4   Tomorrow soud hae been my bonnie waddin day
       If I had staid in London.

5   She turned her aboot, wi an angry look.
       An' sic an angry woman –
     Gin tomorrow soud hae been your bonnie waddin
       Gae back to your miss in Lunnon.   [day,

6   For mony a day an year, that lady lived in care,
       An' doctors wi her dealin:
     Till just in a crack, her very heart did brak.
       An' her letters went on to Lunnon.

7   There waur four an' twenty o' the noblest lords
       That Lonnon could aford him.
     A' clead in black, frae the saidle to the hat,
       To convey the corpse o' Peggy Ewan.

                . . . .

8   "I'd rather hae lost a' the lands o' Aboyne,
       "Than lost my pretty Peggy Ewan."

31

As The King lay musing on his bed   (Mrs Harris)
[Child no. 164 King Henry Fifth's Conquest of France]

f. 43[v]

no. 25 [26]

The King lay mus- ing on his bed, He thought him - self up -

on a time, Of tri - bute that was due from France, Had

not been paid, for so long a time, Fal - al the day, Fal the rad - dy day.

1   As The King lay musing on his bed,   f. 24[r]
     He thought himself upon a time.   no. 22
   Of tribute that was due from France;
     That had not been paid for so long a time.
       Fal all the day fal the raddy day.

139

2   He callèd on his trusty page –
    His trusty page, then callèd he –
    Says, "you'll go to the king of France,
      "And you'll fall low on your bended knee.
        Fal all &c

3   "My Master greets you worthy sire,
    "Ten ton of gold that is due, to he,
    "And if you do not pay him the same,
      "That in French land, you will soon him see."
        Fal ral &c

4   Away then went the trusty page,
    The trusty page, then away went he;
    Until he came to the king of France,
      When he fell low on his bended knee.
        Fal all &c

5   'My Master greets thee, worthy Sire,
    'Ten ton of gold, that is due to he,
    'And if you do not pay him the same;
      'That in French land, you will soon him see.'
        Fal all .

6   "Your masters young, and of tender age.
    "Not fit to come unto my degree.
    "I'll send him o'er ten tennis balls.
      "He's fitter for to learn to play.'
        Fal all &c –

7   Away then went the trusty page,
    The trusty page then away went he.
    Until he came to our gracious king.
      When he fell low on his bendèd knee.
        Fal all. &c.

8   'He says you're young and of tender age.
        'Not fit to come unto his degree –
      'He'll send you oe'r ten tennis balls,
        "You're fitter for to learn to play – '
            Fal all &c

9   Recruit me then in Lincolnshire;   f. 24ᵛ
        They of the Derby hills so free.
      Niether married man, nor widow's son:
        For the widow's curse shall not go with me.
            Fal all &c

10   They recruited then, in Lincolnshire.
        They of the Derby hills so free –
      Niether married man, nor widow's son.
        They were a jovial companie.
            Fal all &c

11   Up they marched and in to France,
        Wi drums an' trumpets merrilie;
      When up he spoke the King of France,
        "Lo yonder comes proud Henerie!"
            Fal all &c.

12   The first shot that the English gave –
        Of the French men they killed so free –
      While up he spoke the King of France –
        "Have mercy on my men and me."
            Fal all &c

13   "And you shall have the tribute home.
        "The tribute that is due to thee.
      "Of all the flowers, that grow in France.
        "The Rose of England, shall go free – "
            Fal all the day fal the Raddy day –

141

32

I wald be very sorry   (Miss Seymour
[Child no. 93 Lamkin]   Lethnot)

f. 27ᵛ   1   I wald be very sorry,
no. 28   To wash a basin clean;
             To haud my mithers heart's blude,
             Thats comin, an' I ken.

. . . .

33

Hey for the Birds o Benothie   (Mrs Harris)

f. 28ʳ   1   Hey for the Birds o Benothie
no. 30   An' hou for the Bissats o Ferald –

. . . .

I have been unable to obtain more of this ballad than the chorus. The castle of the Bird family stood on the farm of Couttie parish of Bendochy – near Coupar Angus. There is a monument in this parish church to one of the Birds, a knight in armour. He is said to have been a Crusader. Tradition also relates, that one of that family a very beautiful young Lady, was sent every morning to traverse the Kirkyaird, repeating all the while –

I sae bounie, I sae ried,
Maun I lie doun amang the died?

There was also a Brownie at the Castle – The following rhyme may refer to him – it used to be given as a puzzle to repeat fast.

The cruikit, kuikit cakes o' Couttie,
Raise oot o' the ace nookie;
Says gie's a new cloutit cloutie:
To mend my blue cloutit cloakie.

34

Mosey, Mare   (Wilson a Servant –
                                at Fearn Manse)

f. 28^r
no. 31

1   Mosey was a little man, a clever mare did buy
     She winkèd, she blinkèd, no man could come her
                                        [nigh
     She was as cunning as a fox, as clever as a hare,
     And I will tell you bye and bye, how Mosey catched
                                        [his mare.

2   Mosey in the morning rase, to catch his mare asleep,
     And round about the frosty knowes he on his knees
                                        [did creep.
     He saw her mumping in a ditch, was glad to find her
                                        [there.
     And flang a belt about her middle, so Mosey catched
                                        [his mare.

                    . . . .

3   Salt seasons all things, says Solomon the wise,
     "He that gets a good wife, gets a goodly prize.
     "But he that gets a bad one, falls into a snare.

                    . . . .

143

35

Lord Revel   (Mrs Molison
[Child no. 75 Lord Lovel]   Dunlappin)

f. 28^V   1   Lord Revel he stands in his Stable door,
no. 32   He was dressing a milkwhite steed.
              A lady she stands in her bour door,
                A-dressin with haste an speed.

           2   "Oh where are you gaen? Lord Revel, she said,
              "Where are you going from me?"
              'Its I am going to Lonnon toun –
                That fair city for to see.

           3   "When will you be back? Lord Revel? she said.
              "When will you be back to me'."
              I will be back in the space of three years,
                To wed you my gey ladie.

           4   "That's too long a time for me she said,"
              "Thats too long a time for me."
              "For I'll be dead long time ere that."
                "For want of your sweet companie."

           5   He had not been in Lonnon toun,
              A month but barely three,
              When word was brought that Isabell
                Was sick an' like to dee.

           6   He had na been in Lonnon toun,
              A year but barely ane.
              When word was brought from Lonnon toun
                That Isabell was gane.

           7   He rode, and he rode along the high way.
              Till he came to Edinborrow toon
              "Is there any fair Lady dead?" said he,
                "That the bell gie such a tone?"

8   Oh! Yes there's a ladie, a very fine ladie,   f. 29^r
        Her name it is Isabell –
     She died for the sake of a young Scottish Knight
        His name it is Lord Revel.

9   'Deal, well, deal well, at Isabell's burial,
        'The biscuit and the beer,
     'An' Gainst the morrow at this same time,
        'You'll aye deal mair, and mair.'

10   'Deal well, deal well at Isabell's burial,
        'The white bread and the wine,
     'An' gainst the morn at this same time –
        'You'll deal the Same at mine."

11   They dealt well, dealt weel at I[s]abell's burial,
        The biscuit an' the beer,
     An' gainst the morn at that same time,
        They dealt them mair, an' mair.

12   They dealt weel, dealt weel at Isabell's burial,
        The white bread an' the wine,
     An' gainst the morn at that same time –
        They dealt the same again.

36

Prince Robert   (Mrs Molison)
[Child no. 87 Prince Robert]

f. 29^r   1   Prince Robert he has wedded a wife;
no. 33   An' he daurna bring her hame.
                   The queen . . . .
                   His Mither was much to blame.

                   . . . .

         2   It is the fashion in oor countrie, mither
             I dinna ken what it is here.
             To like your wife better than your mither –
             That   bought you sae dear.

f. 29^v   3   She called upon her best Marie,
                   An' tippet her wi a ring
                   To bring to her the rank poison –
                   To gie Prince Robert a dram.

         4   She put it to her cheek, her cheek:
             She put it to her chin.
             She put it to her fause, fause lips
             But ne'er a drap gaed in.

         5   He put it to his cheek, his cheek:
             He put it to his chin –
             He put it to his rosy lips,
             An the rank poison gaed in.

         6   "Whare will I get a bonnie boy,
             "Wha will win meat an' fee?
             "Wha will rin on to   bower,
             "Bring my gude ladie to me?"

7   'Here am I a bonnie boy,
      'Willin' to win meat an' fee.
    'Wha will rin on to   bower,
      'An Bring your gude ladie.

8   "Whan you come to broken brig,
      "Tak aff your coat an' swim;
    "An' whan you come to grass growin',
      "Tak aff your shoon an' rin."

9   An whan he cam to broken brig,
      He coost his coat an' swam.
    An whan he cam to grass growin,
      Set doon his feet an' ran.

10   An whan he cam to the ladie's bower,
      He fand her a' her lane.

. . . .

11   An syne she kissed his wan, wan lips,

. . . .

37

I'll Gar our gudeman trow   (Mrs Harris)

1   I'll gar oor gudeman trow.   f. 30^r
      That I'll tak the flingstrings   no. 34
    Gin he dinna buy to me,
      Twall gey goold rings;
    Ane to ilka finger,
      An' twa to my thoom.
    Sae stan' aboot ye cummers a'
      An' gie my goon room.

2   I'll gar oor gudeman trow,
      That I'll ding doon the corse.
    Gin he dinna buy to me,
      A braw young pacin horse,
    A braw young pacin horse,
      To ride baith up an' doon,
    Sae stan' aboot ye cummers a'
      An' gie my goon room.

3   I'll gar oor gudeman trow,
      That I'll brak the ladle,
    Gin he dinna buy to me –
      A braw new ridin saidle;
    A braw new ridin saidle,
      To ride baith up an doon;
    Sae stan' aboot ye cummers a'
      An' gie my goon room.

4   I'll gar oor gudeman trow,
      That I'll loup owre the kirk,
    Gin he dinna gie to me,
      A braw new ridin skirt.
    A braw new ridin skirt,
      To ride baith up an' doon.
    Sae stan' aboot you cummers a'
      An' gie my goon room.

38

Oh! Mither I hae a batchelor been   (Mrs Harris)

f. 30^v   1   "Oh! mither I hae a batchelor been,
no. 35   "For Aucht an' forty year;
        "An Meg she says she winna hae me,
        "For as aft at her as I speer."

2   'You'll kaim your head, an' wash your face;
      'An' try her owre again.
    'Gae in to the hoose, an' look unco crouse;
      'An' say a' the braw things that you can.'

3   "Deed Mither, I'm sure, Ise do't
      "As sune's I get oot the muck.
    "But I needna fash, my hands to wash,
      "For muck bodes aye gude luck."

4   His Sunday's coat the youth he put on,
      A blue bonnet wi a ried ring.
    A horn mill, wi sneeshen did fill.
      An' awa to her he did gang.

5   "Hoo are you my little wee doo?
      "My canty bit smootrekin moose.
    "An' hoo's your father, an hoo's your mither,
      "An' a' the gude folks o' the hoose?"

6   "I needna be shamed to shaw you my chin,
      "For brawly you ken my errand.
    "Sae you maun gang away wi me,
      "An' be married yoursel, Ise warrant.

7   "I needna be shamèd to shaw you my shins –
      "Tho' I wat, they're no very lang.
    "Sae you maun gang awa wi me,
      "An' awa wi me ye *maun* gang."

8   '*Maun* was made for the King o' Man,   f. 31^{r}
      'An' for nae ither bodie.
    'Ye micht ee'n said, "wi your will, Fair Maid."
      'An' latten your *maun*'s abe."

9   See-na how she sneers, an' snarls;
      Girns an' gies him the scorn.
    "I think wha buckles wi you young lass,
      "Will no need to lie lang i' the morn."

10   Whan he saw that Meg was awa,
         A-skippin outowre the knowe.
      He dichted his cheeks, an' he blubbered an' grat –
         An' against the stane rappit his pow –

11   Oot cam his Mither, wi her the dish-cloot,
         An' she rubbit it owre his mou.
      The waes i the chiel, I think he's gaen wrang.
         Get up, you bletherin sou.

39

                A wee bittie East there leeved a man   (Mrs McKenzie
                                                                 Borry)

f. 31^r   1   A wee bittie East, there leevèd a man –
no. 36   O' sillar an' sense no that riffie:
                He thocht he'd be married if he can –
                   An' he swoor he soud hae a bit wifie.

           2   A wee bittie wast there leeved a man,
                   O Sillar an' Sense he had plenty.
                Three dochters had he, an' "o' me –
                   The best o' them a' micht be vauntie."

           3   He put on the best o' his blues,
                   An' scrappit doon his beard wi a whottle,
                A mill wi sneeshin he did fill,
                   An' he thocht that she culd not refuse him.

f. 31^V   4   When he cam to the gentleman s door,
                   He did not know the fashions o' the gentry –
                He leant a' his wieght and thrice more.
                   An' lichtit wi' a blad in the entry.

150

5   Servants an' maidens cam rinnin to see,
      An' to goup an' to gaze upon Johnnie –
    But he fexèd his een on Miss Jean;
      An' vowed she was wonderful bonnie.

6   "I hae a gude hoose o' my ain,
      "A weel gaen knock an' an amrie,
    "Twa timmer caups an' some bowls,
      "An' I brak them richt aft whan angry."

7   Miss Jean to carry on the sport.
      She oxtered him ben to the chamber,
    An' aye as he lilted, an' he sang,
      He declared that her een shone like amber.

40

Tod Lowrie   (Mrs Harris
                            & others)

f. 43^V

no. 27 [28]

f. 31ᵛ   1   The tods wife is lyin' sick –
no. 37   Wi seven young tods at her feet.
                 She longed for a bit o' the pykan meat.
                    A' for her lyin in O.

           2   Tod Lowrie cam to oor corn yaird,
                 Says Geese an Ganners ye may be feared;
                 The fattest o' you sall criesh my beard:
                    Or I gae frae the toon O.

           3   The Gude Grey Goose heard word o' that,
                 An' she crap in ahint a stack.
                 "I wis' said she, "I may never be fat.
                    For the Tod has come to the toon O."

           4   Tod Lowrie cam to his tod hole:
                 An' blew his horn loud an' shrill.
                 A Gude Grey Guse is at your will,
                    Unto your lyin in O.

41

Hark Niebour here   (Adam Duncan
Brechin)

f. 44^V
no. 30

Hark, neigh - bour here, a wee and speak, Here is a house that

ne'er saw reek, Its A'___ close a - boot the lum, Sure -

ly this house be - langs to some, Sure - ly this hoose be - langs to some.

1 Hark niebour here, a wee an' speak. f. 32^V
 Here is a hoose, that ne'er saw reek. no. 9
 Its a' close aboot the lum.
 Surely this hoose belangs to Some.
 Surely this hoose belangs to Some.

153

2   Does ghaists or bogles mak a din,
       Aboot the back o't or within.
       Deed kind sir I canna tell –
       Yonder's the lad, spier at himsel,
       Yonder's &c –

3   Hark niebour here a-wee an' lean,
       Upon this dyke, its dry and clean,
       An' tell me the reason, an' the cause,
       Nae-body bides within these wa's.
       Nae-body &c.

4   Indeed kind sir, to tell you true,
       I dinna ken the way to woo.
       An' Lasses are na easy tane –
       An' I dinna like to bide my lane.
       An' I dinna. &c.

5   Tut man, that winna do ava,
       Whaur ane wad sair, you micht get twa,
       An' lasses are no very scant –
       For mony a lass, a lad does want.
       For mony &c.

6   But tent you man to my advice.
       You'll tak nae ane, that's proud an' nice.
       Nor yet tak ane, wi a heap o' sillar,
       If that be the motive, leads you till her –
       If that. &c

7   For Sillar maks a blinkin bride.
       Does mony a faut an' failin hide.
       Yet afterwards they will appear.
       Whan folk begin to tine thier gear.
       Whan folk

8   An' beauty too, its but skin deep –
         Leads many a puir man aff his feet.
         Yet by an bye he weel does know –
         That beauty it is but a show –
         That beauty &c –

9   But virtue is the thing will do,
         An' thats the Lass that ye maun loe.
         For sense an' worth will still remain.
         When wealth an' beauty baith are gane.
         When wealth – &c –

10   Then fare ye weel, I maun awa –
         Ye'll tak nae ane that gaes owre braw.
         But tak the Lassie, that's young an' douce –
         An' bring her in to that toom hoose –
         An' bring &c

11   But stop noo man, be no sae nice,
         Till I thank you for your kind advice.
         For if I hadna met in wi you –
         I wad never kent, the way to woo
         I wad &c

12   But the niest time that ye gae bye,
         Ye'll see my lum reek to the sky –
         An' to your Supper ye'll get a hen –
         An' Sleep a nicht i' the bed there ben –
         An &c –

42

Molly Hustan   (Mrs Harris)

f. 43ʳ
no. 23

1   Late at night, there I spied   f. 33ʳ
          A barefoot maid, trip oe'r the Street.   no. 40
        Oh! the ground shone around –
        With her tender ivory feet.

2   Coal black hair, without compare
          Glittering round her snow white neck.
        Sparkling eyes like morning stars,
          Might save a sinking ship from wreck.

3   Men an' Maids, on her wait,   f. 33ᵛ
         To guard her from all injurie –
      She's the prize, of mine eyes;
         Of all the girls, I now do see.

4   Then at night, it was my care,
         Under her window for to creep –
      To see if she would pity me –
         An' waken from her tender sleep.

. . . .

5   Oh! begone, oh! young man,
         Lest my father should you hear.

6   Doun by the burn, was my return –
         To see my love trip oer the plain –
      Make my bed, tie my head.
         Tell my true love I am slain.

7   She's the fairest, she's the rarest,
         She's the loveliest of this land.
      She's so neat, and so complete,
         I long to take her by the hand.

8   M. and O. bid me go –
         L and Y these lines do grace.
      H. and U bid me rue,
         That ee'r I saw her bonny face.

9   S. and T. bid me stay,
         Patient be and take my ease:
      O and N make an end
         Spell her name now if you please.

The heroine of this song was the daughter of respectable parents, in humble life, a resident of St Andrews about the beginning of the Century. Her lover, a young English gentleman of high connection, attending the University,

157

whose advances she refused, pined away with vexation, fell into consumpt-
ion, and died. A relative of Mrs Harris in St Andrews informed her he had
seen Molly – a very elegant, beautiful woman, modest and without
reproach.

43

Cronnen's Song   (Mrs Harris)

f. 34^r 1   In Paradise I am again,
no. 41 [42]   There's objects here inspire my view,
               And if I your favour still retain.
                 You'll find I'm still a sailor –

        2   And now since I am in this Place
               A sailor's coat I'll ne'er disgrace
               And I hope to see a smile on each female face.
                 You'll find I'm still a sailor.

        3   Both high and low, and each degree –
               You'll find them all the same to me.
               For I walk by the golden rule of three.
                 You'll find I'm still a sailor.

Note.
     This eccentric Laird had served in the navy. He plumed himself on that,
and on acting honourably as a J.P. He so displeased a lady friend, that she
for several years cut him out of her new years parties, which he much
enjoyed. On the third year he arrived at her house without invitation – threw
open the door, and sang the the [sic] above as he advanced.

44

Gentle Johnnie Ogilvie the knicht o' Inverwharity

1   "Gentle Johnnie Ogilvie the knicht o' Inverwharity
      You'll go frae my window you'll go –
      The wind an' the rain theyve turned my love again
      So you'll go frae my window you'll go."

45

In Cortachy Cottage

1   In Cortachy Cottage there lives a young lassie
      A Lassie that I like wondrous fine –
      She's blithe an' she's bonnie, she's far frae saucy –
      An' oh! thinks I if she waur but mine.

2   The first time I saw her was by Esk water –
      The mavis sang sweet, in Cortachy den.
      I gazed with rapture, upon the sweet creature.
      An' Oh! thinks I if she waur but mine –

. . . .

46

They ca' me Nelly Douglas butt the hoose

f. 34^v   1   They ca' me Nelly Douglas butt the hoose,
no. 44 [45]   They ca' me Nelly Douglas ther ben.
               But I will laugh at the best o' them a'
                 To ca' me Nelly Douglas again.

        2   My mither was the cow-herd's wife –
                 My faither wore the plaidie –
               I gaed up the stair a silly servant maid.
                 An' Cam doon Madam an' Ladie.

. . . .

47

Kemp, kemp my Johnnie Soutar

f. 34^v   1   Kemp, kemp my Johnnie Soutar,
no. 45 [46]   An' ye sall get my shoon.
               There wattit wi ried on ilka side.
                 An' giltit wi goud aboon.

. . . .

48

There s buckies i' bog, there's gairies i' glen   (old Lady
from the
Border)

f. 34^v

1   There s buckies i' bog, there's gairies i' glen.   no. 46
Sing Buckies again, sing buckies again.   [47]

. . . .

49

She's a wrang for the richtin ot   (old Lady
from the
Border)

1   She's a wrang for the richtin ot –   f. 34^v
She s a wrang for the richtin ot –   no. 47
[48]

. . . .

50

Hey Tutti taitie   (Mrs Harris)

1   Hey tuttie taitie,   f. 35^r
Hey toutie totie   no. 48
Hey toutie taitie,   [49]
 Wha's fou nou.

2   You'll mak to me some warm drink.
     Some warm drink, some warm drink.
     You'll mak to me some warm drink.
       O' butter, spice an' ale –

3   There's a coo, an' a calf Jean,
     A mare an' a foal Jean,
     The needle i' the wa' Jean,
       An' dinna beguile yoursel.

. . . .

In old times there was only one needle or elson in a Scotch peasant house,
which was stuck in a *divot* or *feal* of the building. A boy at Family worship bawled out during prayer, Father I see the Elson – Wheesht said the
patriarch, but keep your ee' on the Elson.

51

The Ghaist o' Fern Den

f. 35^r   1   There lived [a] farmer in the north,
no. 49 [50]   I canna tell you when –
                 But Just he had a famous farm –
                   No far frae Fearn den.

            2   The muckle Ghaist, the fearfu' ghaist.
                   The Ghaist o' Fearn Den –
                 He wad hae wracht as muckle wark.
                   As four an' twenty men.

            3   If there was ony strae to thrash –
                   Or ony byres to clean.
                 He never thocht it muckle fash.
                   In workin' late at ee'n.

4   Ae nicht the mistress o' the hoose,
      Grew sick an' like to dee;
    An' for a canny wily wife –
      Wi' might and main did cry –

5   The nicht was dark, an' no a spark.
      Wad venture through the glen –
    For fear that they wad meet the ghaist.
      The ghaist o' Fearn Den.

6   But Ghaist he stude ahint the door;
      An' hearin' a' the strife.
    She saw tho' they had men a score;
      They sune wad tyne the wife.

7   Aff to the stable, then he gaed
      An' saidled the auld mare.
    An' through the glush, an' slush he ran,
      Just like ony hare.

8   He chappit at the Mammy s door,
      Says he, "Mak haste an' rise.
    'Put on your claes, an' come wi' Me,
      'An' tak na nae' surprise.'

9   "Whare am I gaen?" quo the wife.
      "Nae far but through the glen.
    "You're wantit to a farmer's wife
      'Nae far frae Fearn Den.'

10 He's taen the Mammy by the hand.
      An' set her on the pad.
    Got on afore her an' set aff;
      As though they baith waur mad.

11 They spieled the braes, they lap the burns.
      An' through the wet did splash.
    They never minded stock, nor stane.
      Nor ony kind o' trash.

163

12   Whan they waur near their journey s end.
       An' scuddin though the glen.
    Then says the Mammie to the ghaist.
       "Oh! are we near the den?"

f. 36ʳ   13   For oh! I'm fleyed we meet the ghaist –
       "Tut! wheesht you fule, quo he.
    For waur than ye hae in your arms –
       This nicht ye sanna see.

14   Whan they cam to the farmer's door,
       He set the Mammie doon.
    "I've left the hoose but ae half hour,
       "I am a clever loon."

15   'What maks your feet sae braid?' quo she.
       'What maks your een sae sair?'
    Quo he, I've wandered mony a nicht.
       Without either horse or mare.

16   But stap in bye, an' mind the wife,
       An' see that ye do richt.
    An' I will tak you hame again.
       At twal o'clock at nicht.

17   An' gin they spier, wha brocht you here,
       'Cause they waur scarce o' men,
    You'll tell them that you rade ahint –
       The Ghaist o' Fearn den.

Note.

    Recently a large stone was removed from the public road, near the Kirk of Fearn. A mark round the middle, was said to have been caused by the "Brownie' struggling so hard to break the cart-rope with which he was bound to the stone, that it sunk into it and remained – He was afterward "conjured" by the son of the farmer's wife, he had so kindly befriended – My Father gave Mr Jervise a copy of the ballad who inserted it in the 'Lands of the Lindsays'.

52

The Battle of La Hogue   (Mrs Harris)
[MUSIC ON FOLLOWING PAGES]

f. 37^r
no. 50 [51]

1   Twas Monday in the Morning the nineteenth of May
     Recorded for ever, the famous ninety two.
   Brave Russel did discern by the breaking of the day
     The Lofty sails of France advancing to.
   "All hands aloft,' he cried; let British valour shine,
  " Let fly a culverine, the signal for the Line.
       'Let every man supply his gun,
        Follow me; you shall see,
       That the battle it shall soon be won

2   Tourville on the main, triumphant rolled,
     To meet the gallant Russel, in combat on the deep –
   He led a noble train of heroes bold;
     To sink the English Admiral at his feet.
   Now every gallant mind to Victory doth aspire,
   The bloody fights' begun, the Sea's all fire.
       The mighty fates are looking on,
        Whilst a flood, all of blood
       Fills the Scuppers of the "Rising Sun".

3   Sulphur smoke and fire, disturbing the air,
     With thunder and wonder affright the Gallic corps
   Their desolated bands, all trembling stand;
     To see their Lofty Streamers now no more.
   See how they fly amazed! through rocks and sand,
   Each danger they grasp at, to shun the greater fate
       Death and horror equal riegn
        Whilst they cry – "run and die",
       British colours ride vanquished main.

165

f. 44ʳ
no. 29

Twas Mon - day in the morn - ing the nine - teenth of May, Re -
cor - ded for ev - er the fam - ous nine - ty two, Brave
Rus - sel did de - cern, By break - ing of the day, The lof - ty sails of France ad -
vanc - ing to. All hands a - loft, he cried, Let Brit - ish val - or shine. Let
fly a cul - ver - ine, The sig - nal for the line Let ev - ery man sup - ply his gun,
Fol - low me, you shall see, That the Bat - tle, it will now be won.

Fig. 4 "Russells Triumph or thee Memorable Ninety two"

(77)

the Memorable Ninety two

Tourville on the main triumphant rowl'd
To meet the gallant Russel in combat oer the deep.
He led his noble troops of heros bold,
To sink the English Admiral and his fleet
Now every gallant mind to victory does aspire
The bloody fight's begun, the sea is all on fire,
    And mighty fate stood looking on;
    Whilst the flood, all with blood,
    Fill the scuppers of the rising Sun.

Sulphur smoak and fire disturbing the air;
With thunder & wonder affright the Gallic Shore.
Their regulated bands stood trembling near,
So see their lofty Strutmers now no more.
At Six o'clock the red, the jading victors led
To give the Second blow the total overthrow;
    Now death and horror equal reigns;
    Now they cry, Run or die,
    Brittish colours ride the vanquish'd main.

See they fly amaz'd o'er rocks and sands,
One danger they grasp to shun a greater fate;
In vain they cry'd for aid to Weeping winds.
The nymphs and sea gods mourn their lost estate.
For evermore adieu thou ever during Sun;
From thy untimely end thy Master's fate begun.
    Enough thou mighty god of war,
    Now we sing & tole the song,
    Let us drink to every English tar.

For the German Flute

53

There cam a Ghost   (Mrs Harris)
[Child no. 77 Sweet William's Ghost]

f. 39ʳ

no. 2

There cam a Ghost to Mar - git's door, Wi mo- ny a griev- ous groan, An

lang it___ tir - led at the pin, But an - swer___ made it none.

54

Benonie   (Mrs Harris
[Child no. 10 The Twa Sisters]   and others)

f. 40^V
no. 11

Oh! Sis - ter, sis - ter,   tak me out ag-en!   No - nie, an' Be - no - nie But

wi a sil-ler cane, She shot her far-er in, to the bon-nie mill dam o' Be - no - nie.

55

Babie Allan   (Mrs Harris
[Child no. 84 Bonny Barbara Allan]   & others)

f. 41^r

no. 14

It fell a-boot the Mart-mas time, When green leaves they war fal-lin; That Sir John Graham o' the North Kin-trie, Fell in love wi Baw-bie Al-lan.

56

Hie Marshall   (Anne Skain)

f. 42^v

no. 21

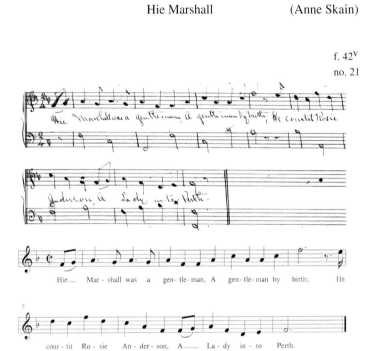

Hie— Mar - shall was a gen - tle - man, A gen - tle - man by birth; He

cour - tit Ro - sie An - der - son, A— La - dy in - to Perth.

57

Young Becon   (Mrs Harris)
[Child no. 53 Young Beichan]

f. 43^V
no. 26 [27]

Young Be-con was our Cap-tain's name, He was a tall and stout young man, As

bold a Sai-lor as sailed the sea, And we were bound for New Bar - bar - y.

58

Hech, Hey, Lowrie lay   (Mrs Harris)

f. 44^r
no. 28

Whaur will we tak up oor hoose? Hech, hey, Low - rie lay,

Quo' the pad - dock to the moose, Wi a row - ly pow - ly,

gu - ger - ly gow - ly, Gu- ger - ly gow, an' oor lad - die.

59

There we left her   (Mrs Harris)
(Gaelic air)

f. 44^V
no. 31
[repeated
no. 30]

NOTES

After the number and title or titles in this edition, the notes give the Child number and title or a reference to the occurrence of the song in another collection when this is known. The music notes indicate other publications derived from MS B, the tune tradition to which each air belongs, if available, and any unusual editorial decisions made in transcribing the tune. In each case, the general form of the tune is indicated in alphabetic letters, and its tonic and tonal content with standard symbols in parentheses (♭7 = flatted seventh degree; -4 = missing fourth degree, etc.); if there is no indication, the tune is fully heptatonic and in the major. The range is indicated by showing in square brackets the lowest to the highest note used (with c = middle c; c' an octave higher; C an octave lower). The textual notes refer separately to MSS A and B.

PART 1

1 *Sir Patrick Spens.*

Child 58 *Sir Patrick Spens.*
Music
ABA'C (tonic F; -7) [A-c']. Child 5.415, Bronson no. 5. From comparisons with the thirteen tunes in Bronson, this is closest to those collected in Tennessee and Virginia in the 1930s (his nos 6 and 7).
Text
A: 9.2 "three" follows deleted "five". 9.4 "Cam" is written over "Their" and "gude" is deleted before "driving". 17.1 "Then" is written and deleted nearer the edge of the page than the text and opposite the start of 17.2 and 17.3.
B: 22.4 "sai" of "sailing" altered, probably from "hie"; cf. 23.4 "hieing". 24.3 "Sir" altered from "her"; cf. "her" at 23.3.

2 *Sir Colin.*

Child 61 *Sir Cawline.*
Music
AA'BC (tonic C; -4) [d-e']. Child 5.415, Bronson no. 1. Bronson correctly points out resemblances to the Appalachian tune tradition for

Child 53 *Young Beichan* (cf. Bronson no. 57, collected in Tennessee) and to Child 191 *Hughie Grame* (cf. Bronson no. 4, minus the chorus, collected by Duncan – *GD* 271A).

Text

B: Verses 1, 2, 3 and 5 were written first with verse 4 written below them at the foot of the page under a dividing line. Crosses serving as asterisks indicate that this verse should be inserted between 3 and 5.

3 *Archerdale, The Knicht o' Archerdale.*

Child 47 *Proud Lady Margaret.*

Music

ABCD (tonic D; ♭3, ♭6, ♭7) [d-f']. Child 5.414, Bronson no. 1. Both Bronson and Child halve the note values given in the Harris MS. The tune tradition is a scattered one, according to the three specimens given by Bronson. His guess that the tune could have antecedents in eighteenth-century hymnody is supported by the discovery by Professor Nicholas Temperley, University of Illinois, of three tunes in his computerised Hymn Tune Index which have striking resemblances to at least portions of this one. They are "Gossett" from *Psalmodia Evangelica* (London, 1789); "Epping" from *Psalms and Hymn Tunes Selected for the Use of the Hollis-Street Society* (Boston, 1811); and "Guil[d]ford" by William Tans'ur and found in his *A Compleat Melody* (London, 1735). The two British examples might well have been in circulation in Perthshire and could have been used as part of the melodic material of the tunes as learned by Grace Dow in the late eighteenth century.

Text

A: 7.1 "he" is written "she" with "s" deleted. 17.4 "When it" is altered from "What".

B: 5.4 The quotation marks at the end of the line are partially erased. 14.4 "You will" altered from "You'll".

4 *Sweet Willie, My luve she lives in Lincolnshire.*

Child 256 *Alison and Willie.*

Music

ABCD (tonic E; ♭3, ♭7) [d-f♯']. Child 5.423, Bronson no. 1, only tune. Both Child and Bronson halve the note values given in the MS; the Child version has an error on the first note of the next to last measure. Bronson cites as relatives Child 247 (Bronson 4.13, a "Lady Elspat" version as sung by Mrs Brown of Falkland) and Child 252, no. 3, a tune collected by Greig for *The Kitchie-Boy* (*GD* 1048B). Clearly the former is a very close relative, with some of the larger intervals filled in. The Greig tune relationship is a much more distant one, with most of the distinctive large intervals absorbed into a flatter contour.

Text

B: 2.3 "to" is written "too" with second "o" faint and partly erased. 3.2 "[will]": Child emendation which has the support of MS A. 3.3 "yoursell" altered from "mysell". 5.1 "saiddle" altered from "saidle". 5.3 "mind" altered, possibly from "care". 6.1 "set": Child silent emendation for "sed" in the MS. This reading, confirmed by the parallel at 5.1, has been accepted into the text; the "d" in the word was apparently a slip caused by the proximity of "saiddle". 7.3 "e" of "get" altered from "o". 10.3 "She": Child emendation for "He" in the MS. This reading, confirmed by MS A and the Buchan version, has been accepted into the text.

5 *There Were three Ladies, There waur Three Ladies.*
(Title with the music: *There waur three Ladies in a Ha'.*)

Child 11 *The Cruel Brother.*
Music

ABCD (tonic C) [c-g']. Child 5.412, Bronson no. 1. Both Bronson and Child halve the note values. Bronson mis-transcribes the upbeat in m. 2 as an "a" (and criticises Child for transcribing it correctly). The Harris tune appears to be distantly related to a tune for the ballad collected by Sharp in North Carolina in 1917 (no. 4 in Bronson's grouping), especially after the initial stanza of that tune.

6 *Young Logie.*

Child 182 *The Laird of Logie.*
Music

ABCD (tonic G; ♭3, -6, ♭7) [c-f']. Child 5.421, Bronson no. 1. Bronson points out the resemblance of this tune to that for *Hind Horn* (cf. his Child 17, nos. 8-14) and to the tune often known as "I am the Duke of Norfolk", which appears in Playford's *The English Dancing Master* of 1651 and after as "Paul's Steeple". The first half of that tune has the bare harmonic outline of this tune.

Text

B: 5.2 "You" altered from "Ye".

7 *Young Reedin, Young Riedan.*
(Title with the music: *The Lady stude in her bour door.*)

Child 68 *Young Hunting.*

Music
ABA'C (tonic D) [d-f#']. Child 5.416, Bronson no. 34. Both Bronson and Child halve the note values. Bronson also introduces a fermata sign in the second bar. This tune could be seen as distantly related to Child 200 *The Gypsy Laddie* (cf. Bronson no. 54).

Text
B: 6.2 "her" altered from "him". 12.2 "u" of "glue" altered from "o". 9.4 "Young Riedan [in]": Child emendation which has not been accepted into the text. MS A confirms the MS B reading. 10.3 "[maid]": Child emendation which has the support of MS A.

8 *Glen Logie, There waur Aucht an' forty nobles.*

Child 238 *Glenlogie, or, Jean o Bethelnie.*

Music
While there is no tune given by Jane Harris, the air for this text, according to a note by Amelia Harris, is "Auld Rob Morris", which can be found in Johnson 1789-1803: no. 192. This is not the traditional "Glenlogie" tune. The first half fits the verse well, with the addition of some notes in the first phrase; the second half would have to be left off. Bronson mentions this tune reference.

Text
A: 4.2 This line is written over two crosses which indicated an omission.

9 *Roudesdales.*

Child 246 *Redesdale and Wise William.*

Music
No tune is given by Jane Harris but, according to Amelia Harris, the text is sung to the air "Johnnie Brod", which is no. **13** in this edition. Bronson notes that the air is that of Child 114 *Johnnie Cock* but reports it with this ballad since it is the sole known tune.

Text
A: 9.3 "For" is written over "And" 18.4 The "u" of "bought" is inserted with a caret. 19.3 "your" is written over "my".
B: 4.1 "your": Child emendation for "her" in the MS. This reading, confirmed by MS A, has been accepted into the text. 7.1 This line is

written close to 6.4 and the lines taken here and in Child as 7.1-2 could be regarded as 6.5-6. 7.2 "Wald" first written "Wad" and "l" then superimposed. 10.2 A deleted first minim of "M" appears in the unindented position. 17.2 "it" superimposed on "he".

10 *Johnnie Armstrong.*

Child 169 *Johnie Armstrong.*
Music
ABA'C; could also be analysed as ABCD (tonic A; -4) [B-c♯']. Child 5.420, Bronson no. 7. This editor has followed Bronson and Child in adding a semiquaver "e" at the end of m. 2 to accommodate the word "his" for better accentuation of the phrase "His name was Johnnie Armstrong". In addition, I have also changed note values and moved the bar-line between bars 1 and 2 for the sake of correct word accentuation of the phrase "in the north-west land".

11 *The Earl o' Roslyn's Dochter, Captain Wedderburn.*
(Title with the music: *The Earl o' Roslyn's Dochter.*)

Child 46 *Captain Wedderburn's Courtship.*
Music
ABCD; could also be analysed as AA'BA" (tonic E; ♭7) [e- g♯']. Child 5.414, Bronson no. 8. This editor follows Child and Bronson in moving the first note of m. 9 in the MS to m. 8 in order to improve accentuation of the phrase "A sparrow's horn". In addition I have changed the f♮ at the end of m. 5 to a g♯ to match the parallel place in m. 1, and have added a d♮ in m. 10 to parallel the mixolydian flavour given in mm. 7 and 15 in similar situations. This tune has resemblances in general contour to Bronson variants nos 15-17 for the same ballad, but the relationship is not particularly close.
Text
B: 1.3 "a" altered from "wi"; cf. "wi" in MS A. 11.1 the word "a" appears before "some" and had been deleted in pencil. 12.3 the line ends in ink with "you" but this word had been deleted and "me" substituted by Child. This emendation has been accepted into the text.

12 *The Rose o' Balindie, The Rose o' Malindie O.*

Child 20 *The Cruel Mother.*

Music

ABB'C; could also be analysed as ABCD (tonic A; ♭3, -6, ♭7) [e-e']. Child 5.413, Bronson no. 5. Bronson appears to take his version directly from Child rather than from the MS. Except for the rhythmic changes in m. 3 (using semiquavers instead of quavers to make the count come out right), they both follow the MS, even in its awkward and nonsensical treatment of the words in m. 5. This editor has changed the rhythms in mm. 5-6 to reflect the crotchet patterns already established and to make a stronger accentuation for the word "flour", which Jane Harris perhaps tried to indicate with a mark over the note. The tune begins with a phrase in a downward contour resembling some versions of *The Gypsy Laddie* (cf. Bronson's Child 200, nos 73-7), but ends with the rising fourth characteristic of several tunes for this text (cf. Bronson's Child 20, nos 2-4).

Text

B: 12.1 "welcome eel" is written over "eel i' the", the second "welcome" having been omitted from the opening of the line as first written.

13 *Johnnie Brod.*

Child 114 *Johnnie Cock.*

Music

AA'A''BB' (tonic B♭; -7) [f-f']. Child 5.419, Bronson no. 4. Child makes small changes in the rhythms in bars 4, 8 and 9. This editor and Bronson make more extensive rhythmic changes in mm. 8-9 in order to make textual and musical sense of the phrase, "bands, bands, waur bound wi' iron bands". The melody has a resemblance, already pointed out by Keith, to a version of *The Knight and Shepherd's Daughter* (cf. Bronson's Child 110, no. 16). The ending of the Harris tune resembles other Scottish examples collected in the twentieth century (cf. Bronson nos 9, 10, 13 and 14).

Text

A: 4. 1-2 These two lines are written in where an omission had been indicated by three crosses.

B: 1.5 This line is in small writing and was evidently squeezed in after verse 2 had been begun. 3.4 the "e" of "be" is superimposed on "y". 10.1 "by yonder" is superimposed on "among the". In the note, lines 2-4 of the stanza are written out as verse, but the words given here as the opening line of the stanza are run on as part of the prose. The asterisks are indicated by small crosses, the one in the line of verse coming before and slightly above "cut". Child gives the first line of this independent verse as: "But aye at ilka ae mile's end". However, there is a comma after "but" in the manuscript which suggests that this word is still part of the prose and that the verse line begins with "Aye".

14 *Burd Helen, Burd Hellen, or Broughty Wa's.*
(Title with the music: *Burd Helen, or, Brochtie Wa's.*)

Child 258 *Broughty Wa's.*
Music
ABCD (tonic E♭) [e♭-e♭']. Child 5.423, Bronson no. 1. Both Child and Bronson halve the note values and make the semiquaver and dotted-quaver rhythm in m. 2 into a grace note.
Text
A: 5.2 "win" is written above deleted "get".
B: 1.4 The opening of this line was first written "O' Brochty near". This has been altered to "An' Provost of" and "near" has been scored out. 7.2-4 The wording of verse 8 was first given here and then the lines were partially rubbed out and overwritten by the lines printed. 9.3 In "favour" two letters have been deleted between "a" and "v". 10.1 "It" superimposed on "They".

15 *Charlie Macpherson, Charlie MacPherson.*

Child 234 *Charlie MacPherson.*
Music
While there is no tune given by Jane Harris, the air is listed by Amelia Harris as "Whilk o' ye lasses". This is *GD* 816 "Glowerow-erem", which has a chorus that runs (in version B):

> Whilk o' ye lasses 'ill gang to Balcairn?
> Whilk o' ye lasses 'ill gang to Balcairn?
> Whilk o' ye lasses 'ill gang to Balcairn?
> To be goodwife o' bonny Balcairn?

While the "Glowerowerem" tune carries a humorous text and refrain which seems at odds with the character of this serious ballad, the words can be made to fit the tune with the refrain left out. Bronson omits to mention this tune.

Text
B: 1.1 "lad[die]": Child emendation which has not been accepted into the text. MS A confirms the MS B reading. 3.1, 7.1 In both cases the "a" of "Whan" appears to have been altered from "e". 4.1 "whare [i]s": Child emendation which is not necessary since Amelia Harris uses the space before the "s" to signify an apostrophe. MS A has "Whaur's". 4.2 "socht" is written "sochter" with "er" deleted. 6.2 the letters "ou" of "Muirtoun" are superimposed on other letters, probably "on". 8.2 the "b" of "bricht" altered from "f". 8.3 "she was" replaces partially erased "they waur".

16 *Mary Hamilton, Marie Hamilton.*

Child 173 *Mary Hamilton.*

Music
ABCD (tonic D; ♭3, -6, ♭7) [A-c']. Child 5.421, Bronson no. 5. Both Child and Bronson translate the semiquavers in m. 3 literally; clear enunciation of the text seems to require quavers instead. The pitch content of the opening phrase is strange; this editor has moved it down a third into a more typical pitch configuration.

Text
B: 10.4 "hanged upon" altered from "hangit on".

17 *Sweet William.*
(Title with the music: *My Husband built for me a Bower.*)

Child 106 *The Famous Flower of Serving-Men.*

Music
ABCDCD (tonic F) [f-g']. Child 5.418, Bronson no. 1. Both Child and Bronson change the opening semiquaver to a quaver. As mentioned by Bronson, a tune collected by Duncan in the early twentieth century is the closest relative (cf. Bronson no. 2; *GD* 180B).

Text
A: "Air Young Becon" is written in brackets at the right hand side of the heading: cf. **59**.
B: Verses 4-5, 6-7 and 9-10 are written without space between them. 1.5 "night" altered from "day". 6.6 A line crossing the "l" of "slew" as if it were a "t" has been scribbled out.

18 *Fair Margaret.*

Child 63 *Child Waters.*

Music

AA'BA" (tonic F; ♭3, ♭7) [f-f']. Child 5.415, Bronson no. 1. Both Child and Bronson maintain the strange rhythm of m. 9 which I have chosen to rewrite into conformity with the text and other nearby rhythmic patterns. Likewise, the odd closing, solved in two different ways by Child and Bronson, is offered in a third interpretation.

Text

A: At 3.1 and 4.1 "drink" is altered from "eat"; in the first case it is clear that the alteration was made before the rest of the line was written. The letter read as "t" at the end of the line runs off the edge of the page and is only partially present.

B: 4.1 In "Though" an apostrophe after "o" suggests that the word was first written "tho'". 5.3 "i" of "sigh" altered from "a", cf. "say" later in the line. 6.4 "L" of "Lord" altered from "l". 8.2 "ca'" written "ca's" with "s" deleted. 12.1 "He" altered from "She". 16.3 "Ershe" altered from "Erse". 20.3 "travis" or possibly "traviss" altered from "travesse". 20.4 Child emends "Or" to "Nor", comparing with G14.3-4 "See that his meat be at his head,/ And not among his feet."; his emendation has not been accepted into the text. MS A confirms the MS B reading. 23.2 "u" of "Sune" altered from "oo".

19 *Andrew Cowper, Andrew Coupar.*
(Title with the music: *Andrew Cooper.*)

The only other reference to this song that has been located occurs at page 141 of *The History of Blairgowrie* (MacDonald 1899), where some notes on " Legends, Ballads, &c." include an item headed "Oh, wae's me, Cluny!" which runs as follows.

> There is a legend connected with the district that the laird of Clunie shot the laird of Lochblair dead, in the Churchyard of Caputh, in consequence of the former marrying the sweetheart of the latter. A ballad, of which the following are a few lines, says:–
>
> > Oh wae's me Cluny!
> >   Wi' your ha's an' your towers,
> > You've wedded my Jeanie
> >   Wi' your orchards and flowers.

. . . .

> There's gold in my coffers
> But there's nane in Lochblair.

. . . .

> Bonnie Andro Coupar,
>   His sword out he drew,
> And he swore that thro' Cluny
>   He wad mak' it gae thro'.

This item is followed by one that relates to **33** "Hey for the Birds o Benothie" and it seems not unlikely that these texts and comments were derived from the Harris family.

Music

ABA'B (tonic E) [e-f♯']. The pitches of the first three notes and their parallels in mm. 8-9 have been transposed up a third to make better musical sense. The 7th degree could be flatted to conform better with stylistic norms.

Text

A: The note is superimposed on the line of crosses at the end of this song and on part of the title of the next one.

B: Verses 1 and 2 are written without space between them. 3.1 "w" is written and partially erased after this line. 6.1 The "o" of "Coupar" is superimposed on "l". 7.1 The word "Haud" was apparently originally written "Had".

20 *The Kitchen Boy, The Kitchie Boy.*

Child 252 *The Kitchie-Boy.*

Text

B: 6.1 The "m" of "mask" is written over "o". 8.3 "on" is superimposed on other letters, probably the incompletely written word "by".

21 *Robin, Robin he's gane to the wude.*

Child 277 *The Wife Wrapt in Wether's Skin.*

Music

While no tune is given by Jane Harris, the air is named by Amelia Harris in MS B as "Jo Janet", a tune found in Johnson 1787-1803: no. 111. In this case, the text fits most naturally with the second half of the tune given, with its "Jo Janet" refrain. Bronson includes this tune reference in his notes.

Text

B: 6.3 "[sheep]" is an editorial addition which has the support of MS A; Child emended by adding "[wither]".

22 *Teedle ell O, Robin's Tes'ment.*

Cf. *GD* 646 "Robin's Testament".

23 *Wearies Wells, Wearie's Wells.*

Child 4 *Lady Isabel and the Elf-Knight.* This version of the ballad has been discussed by Holger Nygard (1958: 305-11) and David Buchan (1970).

Text

A: 4.1 "tak aff, tak" is superimposed on "Leave af".

B: 2.3 "[aff]": Child emendation which has been accepted into the text.

24 *Hughie Graham, Hughie Grame.*

Child 191 *Hughie Grame.*

Text

B: "Fragment" is written on the left hand side of the page below the song number. Title: "Grame" is written "Greame" with "e" deleted. 1.2 "hills" altered from "hilles". 1.3 "e" has been inserted and deleted after the "a" of "Grame". The single verse is clearly the opening of the ballad. Omission is indicated after it in both versions.

25 *Brown Edom, Broun Edom.*

(Title with the music: *Brown Edom the Smith.*)

Child 98 *Brown Adam.*

Music

ABCD (tonic D; -4, ♭7) [d-d']. Child 5.417, Bronson no. 2. Child and Bronson make the opening note long, while halving the next two values, as in the MS; the rest of the tune note-values they cut in half.

26 *The Lady o' Arngosk, An' they hae brocht her to a bed.*

Child 225 *Rob Roy*. Cf. also Child 224 *The Lady of Arngosk*.

Text

B: The heading "Fragment" is followed by an asterisk to which the note is appended after the verse. The title printed here is the first line of the verse.

27 *The higher that the mountain is.*

These are verses used in psalm practice. See Reid 1906-11. The following is among the verses quoted by Reid.

> The langer that the ploom tree stands,
> The riper grow the plooms;
> The langer that the souter works,
> The blacker grow his thooms.

Text

A: The title is "Old Song". The title given here is taken from the first line. Amelia Harris says that she got this item from her father, David Harris (letter to Aytoun, 12 November 1859; pp. xviii-xix above).

28 *Hech hiegh Durham.*

Cf. *GD* 645 "The Ram o' Dirram".

Text

A: In the title "Hech" is altered from "Heich". A small dash after "Durham" appears to indicate the end of the title; it is followed by words in brackets which may read "v[er]y Large" but the reading is not certain. Like the previous item, this song was recovered by Amelia Harris from her father (see her letter at pp. xviii-xix).

29 *East Muir King.*

Child 89 *Fause Foodrage*.

Music

ABCD (tonic B; ♭3, -6, ♭7) [d-f♯']. Child 5.416, Bronson no. 1. Child and Bronson halve most of the note values, keeping, however, the upbeats in mm. 1, 2 and 4 at their original values. This modification, as in our edition, makes the rhythmic pattern of the first half of the song consistent with that of the second. I have also modified the rhythm of m. 4 to fill the same time as other measures – a lengthening which Jane Harris may have wanted to indicate with her long mark over the c♯. The only thing which the three tunes for this ballad given in Bronson have in common is their pentatonic or hexatonic configuration. However, the tune collected by G. F. Duncan for *Child Maurice* (cf. Bronson's Child 83, no. 7; *GD* 214 "Gill Morice" A), is very close in contour and mode, as is that for versions of *Sir James the Rose* (cf. Bronson's Child 213, nos 1-12).

Text

B: The asterisks appear as small crosses in the MS, the one in the line of verse occurring under "may".

PART 2

30 *Earl of Aboyne.*
(Title with the music: *The Earl of Aboyne.*)

Child 235 *The Earl of Aboyne.*
Music
ABCD (tonic D; -4) [A-e']. Child 5.422, Bronson no. 3. Child and Bronson modify the rhythm and barring of mm. 4 and 8. Child prints a "g" instead of an "a" for the penultimate note. Bronson puts the notes in m. 7 for the text "o' A -" a third lower. This editor transposes most of m. 5 a third lower to make better musical sense. This tune is definitely related to two other early tunes printed in Bronson (nos 1-2).

Text
3.2 "Haud" altered from "Set".

31 *As The King lay musing on his bed.*
(Title with the music: *The King lay musing on his bed.*)

Child 164 *King Henry Fifth's Conquest of France.*
Music
ABCDE (tonic E) [e-g♯']. Child 5.420, Bronson no. 6. The opening note, which looks like a "d" in the MS, is here interpreted as an "e" for musical sense. Both Child and Bronson use two semiquavers at the end of m. 7 instead of the dotted quaver-semiquaver combination chosen by this editor to interpret Jane Harris's ambiguous notation. Otherwise, the tune is a straightforward version of the tune most frequently found with this ballad (cf. Bronson nos 1-5), ranging from the mid-nineteenth-century British to the twentieth-century Ameri-

can. One of its most persistent features is the downward octave leap in the third phrase.

Text

The MS heading is "English Ballad". The title given here is the first line of the text. 8.2 "his" superimposed on partially erased "my". 12.1 "that" squeezed in between "shot" and "the". This ballad begins a new page and at the top right Furnivall has added the note "(King Henry V's Conquest of France: see *Percy Folio Bal & Rom.* [Hales and Furnivall 1868] ii. 597)".

32 *I wald be very sorry.*

Child 93 *Lamkin.*

Text

The heading is "Fragment". The title printed here is the first line of the verse.

33 *Hey for the Birds o Benothie.*

The following item headed "Hey! an' How!" occurs in MacDonald 1899: 141, after an item on Andrew Coupar (see note to song **19**).

> Part of a refrain of another and older ballad relates also to the neighbourhood, and to two rival families:–
>
> > Hey! the Birds of Benothy! and
> > How! the Bissats of Ferold!
>
> Tradition says that a beautiful daughter of the former was sent daily by her parents to the kirkyard of Bendochy to walk there, to keep her in mind of her mortal change.

Text

The heading is "Fragment". The title printed here is the first line of the piece. In the second verse in the note, "new" in the third line is superimposed on "blue".

34 *Mosey, Mare.*

Cf., for music, *GD* 677 "Mossie and His Meer", and, for full words as well as music, see Ford 1904: 39-42.

Text

There is no space between verses 1 and 2.

35 *Lord Revel.*

Child 75 *Lord Lovel.*

Text

After the title, the note "(Lord Lovel scottified)" has been added in ink by Furnivall. 7.4 Child emends "That the bell gie" to "That the bells gie". His emendation has not been accepted since it seems that "gie" may be a subjunctive. 1.1 "I[s]abell's": Child makes this emendation silently.

36 *Prince Robert.*

Child 87 *Prince Robert.*

Text

5.1, 5.2, 5.3 "He" altered from "She". 5.1 "his" altered from "her". 6.2, 7.3 "Wha" is superimposed on earlier writing, possibly "That". 7.1 "am" superimposed on "will". 7.4 The line starts with "Bring" at the normal indented position and "An" was evidently added afterwards.

37 *I'll Gar our gudeman trow.*

Cf. *GD* 1310 "I'll Gar Our Gudeman Trow".

Text

The verses are given on the MS page in the order 1, 3, 4, 2 but a note at the "pacin horse" verse says "2d" and one at the "ridin saddle" verse says "3d". In verse 1, 3-4 and 5-6 are written as two long lines.

38 *Oh! Mither I hae a batchelor been.*

Cf., for words and discussion, Hecht 1904: 323–4,"Robin's Courtship". It is a Scottish adaptation of an English broadside song called "The Merry Wooing of Robin and Joan, the West-Country Lovers" which appears, e.g., in Day 1987: 4.15. The Scottish form was published in Herd 1776: 2.218-19, accidentally merged with another song, and in Struthers 1819: 2.339-40.

Text

3.2 The beginning of "sune's" is superimposed on "aft". 6.3 "maun" inserted with a caret.

39 *A wee bittie East there leeved a man.*

Text

Title: the "E" of "east" is altered from "W". 1.1 The "E" of "East" is altered from "w". 2.1 the "w" of "wast" is altered from "E". 6.2 "knock" is preceded by the letter "c". 7.4 "He" superimposed on "An'".

40 *Tod Lowrie.*

Cf. *GD* 499 "Father Fox" and Opie 1951: no.171 "A Fox Jumped Up One Winter's Night".

Music

ABCD (tonic G; -4) [d-g']. A variant of the commonly sung "Fox Went to Town", the last phrase is also often found with the commonplace text, "among the leaves so green-o".

41 *Hark Niebour here.* (Title with the music: *Hark neighbour here.*)

Cf. *GD* 1394 "The Teem Wa's".

Music

ABCDE (tonic D) [d-e']. In the MS, the first line of this tune seems to be written a third too high; it makes more melodic sense if grounded in the tonic at the beginning, as I have transcribed it. It has a rather distant relationship to the tunes of *GD* 1392; only the second phrase of version B is closely related melodically.

Text

2.1 "or" is superimposed on "an". 5.2 "wad" is superimposed on "micht".

42 *Molly Hustan.* (Title with the music: *Mary Houston.*)

Cf. Kinsley: 1968: no. 226 and Low 1993: no. 95 "O Mally's meek, Mally's sweet." Although this song was attributed to Robert Burns and published among his works, Low commented (p. 291) that it "may well belong to the group of traditional songs revised by Burns". The occurrence of this version in the Harris repertoire and the context given to it there confirm the view that the song was not composed by Burns.

Music

ABCD (tonic F; -3, -7) [c-f']. The opening octave leap, as well as the forthright 4/4 and the very bold contour, which is shared with the previous tune in the music MS, "Andrew Couper"(**19**), argue for an instrumental origin for this tune, though none has yet been found.

43 *Cronnen's Song.*

44 *Gentle Johnnie Ogilvie the knicht o' Inverwharity.*
Cf. Chappell 1859: 1.140-2, "Go from my window, love, go" and Buchan 1828: 2.210, "The Cuckold Sailor".

45 *In Cortachy Cottage.*
Text
1.2 "fine" superimposed on other letters, possibly "weel". 1.5 "k" in "Esk" superimposed on a letter with a downstroke. There is no space between the verses.

46 *They ca' me Nelly Douglas butt the hoose.*
Cf., for words, Buchan 1828: 2.144-5, "The Laird o' Meldrum and Peggy Douglas", and Ord 1930: 123, "Nellie Douglas".
Text
"Fragm[en]t" is written at the top left of the song above the number. The title is taken from the first line. There is no space between the verses.

47 *Kemp, kemp my Johnnie Soutar.*
Text
"Fragm[en]t" is written at the top left of the song, above the number.

48 *There s buckies i' bog, there's gairies i' glen.*
Text
This and the following item have a single comment in the margin: "Snatches of songs sung by old Lady from the Border in 1825". The titles printed here are the first lines of the fragments.

49 *She's a wrang for the richtin ot.*
Text
See note to **48**.

50 *Hey Tutti taitie.*
Cf. Johnson 170 "Hey Tutti Taiti", beginning "Landlady, count the lawin" and *GD* 706 "Be Kin' Tae Yer Nainsel, John".

Stanza 1 is written as two long lines. In the note "Family" is inserted with a caret before "worship".

51 *The Ghaist o' Fern Den.*

Cf., for words, *GD* 342 "The Ghaist o' Fernden". Amelia Harris's note about her father at the end of this song is confirmed by a footnote to a different version of "The Ghaist o' Ferne-den" in Gammack (1882: 257) which says: "For this ballad, Mr. Jervise was indebted to the late Rev. Mr. Harris of Fern, who had it from the late Rev. Dr. Lyon of Glamis about 1812-13." A footnote at p. 255 has the detail that, "The *Ghaist's Stane*, or the piece of rock to which that worthy was chained, still lies in the burn in the vicinity of the kirk!" The farmer's wife in the song was said to be "the gudewife of Farmerton" and one tradition ran that her son, at the time of whose birth the "ghaist" had been so helpful, on growing to manhood, spoke to the spirit and "gave him rest" (p. 258). Cf. also Jervise 1853: 203-8.

Text

5.3 "that" superimposed on "they". 6.4 "tyne" altered from "tine". 17.1 "they" superimposed on "you".

52 *The Battle of La Hogue.*

(Title with the music: *Battle of La Hogue.*)

Cf., for words and historical context, see Firth 1908: xliv-ix, 119-20, 346. The battle was fought on 19 May 1692.

Music

ABCDECC'D' (tonic G) [d-e']. The musical notation of this tune, the longest of any of the thirty-one, is fraught with problems, which have been resolved only with a very free interpretation of the rhythmic notation, including using dotted rhythms not clearly indicated (mm. 1, 6, 9, 11, 13), moving bar-lines for correct accentuation (mm. 2, 3, 8, 15), and selectively halving certain note values in nearly every measure. The emphatic nature of the text (and perhaps a hint of the performance practice) is brought out by both the lines and fermatas in the music (mm. 2, 8), but especially by the presence in the last bar of an underlined text – and what appear to be staccato marks in the bass line. The earliest known version of a tune to this text is on a broadside of 1694, an edition found at Harvard University under the title "The Battel at Sea". The tune bears little resemblance to the Harris tune, except in general mood and style; its strongest resemblance is in the last phrase.

Text

3.2 "Gallic" is superimposed on the word "gallant" of which the "t" has been partially erased. 3.6 "Each" has been superimposed on another word, probably "The", and Amelia Harris has clarified the reading by putting an equals sign above the word and noting "= Each" at the bottom of the page.

53 *There cam a Ghost.*

Child 77 *Sweet William's Ghost.*
Music
ABCD (tonic D; -4) [d-f♯'] Child 5.416, Bronson no. 1. Both Child and Bronson halve the note values (except for the quavers in m. 5, which are undoubtedly a mistake and which I have converted to crotchets).

54 *Benonie.*

Child 10 *The Twa Sisters.*
Music
ABA'C (tonic D; ♭3, ♭7) [B-d']. Child 5.412, Bronson no. 14. Child is faithful to the notation as given, except for adding a dot to the crotchet in the last measure. Bronson changes the barring from m. 4 on, as well as changing mm. 4 and 7 into 5/4. This editor changes the barring also for better word accentuation, but leaves the tune in 4/4 throughout. None of the tune versions for this ballad given in Bronson is particularly close, but nos 15, 20, 85, 87 and 88 bear a certain family resemblance.

55 *Babie Allan.*

Child 84 *Bonny Barbara Allan.*
Music
AA'BC; could also be analysed as AA'BB' (tonic A; -4, -7) [e-f♯']. Child 5.416, Bronson no. 79. Child and Bronson halve the note values and Child puts in extra notes to accommodate text syllables in mm. 5 and 6, as does the present editor. This tune is not particularly close to any other "Barbara Allan" variant, although it has a general contour similar to Bronson variants nos 170-188 (no. 181 is perhaps the closest). However, as Bronson points out, it has a stronger kinship with tunes to Child 218 *The False Lover Won Back* (cf. Bronson no. 2; *G D* 974A) and to Christie's tune for *The Earl of Mar's*

Daughter (Child 270) without the ornamental tones and extra two phrases.

56 *Hie Marshall.*

Cf. *GD* 1462 "Rosie Anderson".

Music

ABCD (tonic F: -4) [d-f']. A modified "Come-all-ye" ballad tune of the sort discussed by Phillips Barry (1909). ABCD in form with a low arched first phrase, a second phrase rising to the octave, a third phrase descending from octave to tonic, the last phrase reproducing much of phrase 1, but with an appropriate cadence. *GD* 1462 has versions very close to this one, especially C, and Christie prints a rather distant version of the tune, with bowdlerised words (1876-81: l. 220).

57 *Young Becon.*

Child 53 *Young Beichan.*

Music

ABAC (tonic A♭) [a♭-a♭']. Child 5.415, Bronson no. 94. The semiquavers which both Child and Bronson add in the penultimate measure do not make rhythmic sense with the text; Jane Harris wrote quavers, which I have retained. The fermata on the third note of m. 5, used by both Child and Bronson, is in the MS an ambiguous line (perhaps a slip of the pen), neither straight like the lines on the two preceding notes, nor a clear fermata, as she uses in many other tunes (see the tune for **2**, for example). This tune has a slight resemblance to the tunes to the *Young Beichan* text presented in Bronson as variants 88-93, but it is not a strong relationship. Cf. **17** *Sweet William* where there is a reference to the air of this ballad.

58 *Hech, Hey, Lowrie lay.*

Cf. *GD* 1633 "Ki-Ma-Dearie" and Opie 1951: no. 175 "A Frog He Would A-Wooing Go".

Music

ABAA'C ((tonic D; -4, ♭7)) [f♯-f♯']. The "c♯" suggested in the last bar confirms the D-major tonality which prevails throughout. With its nearly chant-like tune, focussing on the f♯-a third, and its nonsense refrain, this tune is the most like a children's song of any of the collection. It is related in style to *GD* 1633.

59 *There we left her.*

ABAC (tonic D; -7) [B-d']. Designated by Jane Harris as "Gaelic air" and without a text underlay, the tune is written in even minims, as if it were a hymn tune, although no close cognates have been located in that repertoire. Perhaps the choice of minims signified an especially slow tempo, further emphasised by the fermata in bar 3. The Gaelic air "Dhealaich mise 'nochd ri m' leannan" from *A' Chòisir-Chiùil: The St. Columba Collection of Gaelic Songs* (n.d.: 18) is similar in its beginning phrase and part of phrase 2, but then departs melodically.

APPENDIX A

JANE HARRIS'S LISTS OF SONGS

[1] List of Miss Harris' Ballads[1]

Section first – Oldest Ballads

1 Sir Patrick Spens (**1**); 2 East Muir King (**29**); 3 Broun Edom the Smith (**25**); 4 Knicht o' Archerdale (**3**); 5 My Luve she lives &c (**4**); 6 Young Rieden (**7**); 7 Sir Colin (**2**); 8 Rose o' Melindie O' (**12**); 9 Binonie (**54**); 10 Marie Hamilton (**16**); 11 There cam a Ghost (**53**); 12 Bawbie Allan (**55**); 13 There waur three Ladies (**5**).

II

14 Young Logie (**6**); Fair Margit (**18**); Johnnie Armstrong (**10**); 17 Johnnie Brod (**13**); 18 Burd Helen, or, Brochtie[2] (**14**); 19 Earl of Aboyne (**30**); 20 Hie Marshall (**56**); 21 Earl o' Roslen's dochter (**11**); 22 My husband built &c (**17**); 23 Andrew Couper (**19**); 24 Late at night (**42**); 25 Hark niebour here (**41**); 26 O Mither I hae (**38**); 27 Glen Logie (**8**); 28 Rudiesdale (**9**); 29 Invercauld's kitchie boy (**20**); 30 Wearie's Well (**23**); 31 Hughie Graehame (**24**); 32 The Birds o' Bennochie (**33**); 33 Charlie M Pherson (**15**); 34 Robin he's gaen to the wood (**21**); 35 Robin's Tes'ment (**22**); 36 I'll gar oo'r Gudeman troo   (**37**); 37 Tod Lowrie (**40**); 38 Tutti taitie (**50**); 39 Hech ey Lowrie ley (**58**); 40 A wee bittie east (**39**); 41 Hey Durham (**28**); 42 Ghaist o' Fearn Den (**51**); 43 Gentle Johnnie Ogilvie (**44**); 44 The sma' Caiterin (possibly **26**); 45 In Cortachy Cottage (**45**).

---

[1] These three lists in *Harris Letters* 10 are in Jane Harris's hand and were enclosed with Clyne's letter to Child of 27 August 1873 (see introduction, pp. xxv-vii). The editorial numbering of the lists as [1], [2] and [3] is derived from the headings that appear in the *Harris Letters* MS; Jane Harris did not number the lists herself but she gave them in this order. The editorial additions in round brackets give the number of the song in this edition in bold print and also, in lists [2] and [3], give the position of the item in the words or music section of MS B.

[2] Child has, in pencil, deleted "Burd Helen, or," and added "'s Walls" to make the entry read "Brochtie's Walls".

46 The Battle of La Hogue (**52**); 47 The King lay musing (**31**); 48 Mossie was a clever man (**34**); 49 The hirds o' Hamilton [deleted entry, same as 35 Robin's Tes'ment (**22**)].

[2] Note of Old Ballads & Fragments

1 Sir Patrick Spens (**1**, words 1); 2 Sir Collin (**2**, words 2); 3 Archerdale (**3**, words 3); 4 Fair Margaret (**18**, words 8); 5 Young Logie (**6**, words 10); 6 Rudesdale (**9**, words 9); 7 Young Rieden (**7**, words 4); 8 Bird Helen (**14**, words 12); 9 Glen Logie (**8**, words 11); 10 Sweet William (**17**, words 15); 11 Rose o' Malindie (**12**, words 5); 12 The Kitchie Boy (**20**, words 16); 13 Earl of Aboyne (**30**, words 17); 14 Marie Hamilton (**16**, words 6); 15 There were three Ladies (**5**, words 7); 16 Earl o' Roslyn's daughter (**11**, words 14); 17 Hughie Graehame (**24**, words 27); 18 The Burds o' Bennochie (**33**, words 30); 19 Broun Edom (**25**, words 26); 20 Weerie's Well (**23**, words 19); 21 East Muir King (**29**, words 18); 22 Andrew Cooper (**19**, words 20); 23 Charlie M Pherson (**16**, words 21); 24 Johnnie Brod (**13**, words 23); 25 Johnnie Armstrong (**10**, words 24); 26 My Love she lives (**4**, words 12); 27 Robin he's gaen to the Wude (**21**, words 25); 28 The King lay musing (**31**, words 22); 29 Hark nieghbour here (**41**, words 30); 30 Mary Huston (**42**, words 23); 31 I'll gar oor Gudeman trow (**37**, words 34); 32 Oh Mither I hae a Bachelor been (**38**, words 35); 33 A wee bittie east (**39**, words 36); 34 Mosy was a clever man (**34**, words 31); 35 Tod lowrie's come (**40**, words 37); 36 Robin's Tes'ment (**22**, words 38); 37 The Battle of *La Hogue* (**52**, words 50); 38 Ghaist o' Fearn Den (**51**, words 49); 39 Tutti tette (**50**, words 48); 40 Hech ey Lowrie lay (**58**, music 28); 41 Nae Dominie for me; 42 Whaur are ye gaen; 43 Sailor Laddie; 44 The Banks o' the Nile.

[3] List of Ballad Airs

1 Marie Hamilton (**16**, music 9); 2 There cam a Ghaist (**53**, music 2); 3 Broun Edom (**25**, music 10); 4 Young Logie (**6**, music 17); 5 Hay Marshall (**56**, music 21); 6 Johnnie Armstrong (**10**, music 19); 7 My Love she lives (**4**, music 4); 8 Young Riedan (**7**, music 5); 9

There waur three Ladies (**5**, music 13); 10 Fair Margaret (**18**, music 7); 11 The Earl of Aboyne (**30**, music 16); 12 Andrew Cooper (**19**, music 22); 13 Johnnie Brod (**13**, music 18); 14 Sir Patrick (**1**, music 3); 15 Sir Colin (**2**, music 12); 16 Babie Allan (**55**, music 14); 17 The Knicht o' Archerdale (**3**, music 1); 18 Benonie (**54**, music 11); 19 East muir King (**29**, music 6); 20 Burd Ellen (**14**, music 20); 21 The Rose o' malindie O' (**12**, music 8); 22 The Earl o' Roslyn's dochter (**11**, music 15); 23 Late at night (**42**, music 23); 24 My husband built (**17**, music 24); 25 Hark niebour here (**41**, music 30); 26 The King lay musing (**31**, music 25); 27 Brave Russel (**52**, music 29); 28 Young Becon (**57**, music 26); 29 There we left her (Gaelic Air) (**59**, music 31); 30 Tod Lowrie (**40**, music 27); 31 Hech ey Lowrie lay (**58**, music 28); 32 The Duke o' Gordon had &c [deleted entry]; 32 The bonnie Sailor Laddie; 33 A lang cravat; 34 Nae dominie for me; 35 Sailor Laddie; 36 The Banks of the Nile; 37 Feckless Fanny.[3]

---

[3] The last entry was first written in pencil and then overwritten in ink. For discussion of the songs listed which do not appear in the collection, see the introduction, p. xxxv.

APPENDIX B

PETER BUCHAN'S TEXTS FROM MRS HARRIS

Amelia Harris concludes an introductory note in MS B (ff. 1^V-2^r) with a paragraph on Mrs Harris's links with the Brechin poet, Alexander Laing (1787-1857), and with the ballad collector, Peter Buchan (1790-1854).

> It is worth noting, that Mrs Harris and Laing, the Brechin Poet were great friends, and it was from her, that he heard the story on which he founded the tale of "Archie Allan". When travelling with his *pack*, Laing made her acquaintance and having similar tastes, they soon drew to each other. The Poet after business over, presented the M.S. of his last piece, for criticism, and conversed on topics of mutual interest. It was on one of these occasions she related the history of Willie Melville a housecloth weaver at Mayriggs, in the Parish of Bendochy, which so interested Laing, that he trudged away pack on shoulder, musing as he went along, "Hey puir Willie Melville! I hope he's no puir." When catering for Peter Buchan of Peterhead, Mrs Harris also supplied Laing with several Ballads, two of which appeared in Buchan's Collection.

Laing worked in early life as a heckler (flax-dresser) but, after an accident to his right shoulder which left him unable to do this heavy work, he became a packman, and Amelia Harris refers to this stage of his life, which began about 1817.[4] His verse narrative "Archie Allan" was completed in May 1825 and R. A. Smith acknowledged a draft of it in a letter to Laing of 28 March of that year,[5] so placing the meeting with Mrs Harris at which he got the idea for the poem before this date. The 186-line tale recounts the tragic life of Archie Allan, a decent and hard-working man, who, having lost his daughter and then his wife, married again after a period of deep grief and this time was deceived in his wife who

---

[4] Laing 1857: 25-6, in the introduction by George Gilfillan.

[5] Smith's letter of 28 March 1825 and correspondence between Laing on the one hand and Smith, Allan Cunningham and the Reverend James Brewster on the other which show that he was revising the poem until May are in an unpaginated collection, *Alexander Laing of Brechin's Letters*, Houghton Library MS 25242.15*.

turned out to be a ne'er-do-weel who spent all his money and reduced him to a state of complete destitution. One morning, with nothing to eat and with all his credit spent, he took to the road as a beggar and that night he died on the bare floor of the barn which was the only lodging he had been offered. The opening of the poem runs (Laing 1827: 3):

> Ay! – poor Archie Allan – (I hope he's nae poor,
> A mair dainty neebour ne'er entered ane's door) –
> An' he's worn awa frae an ill-doin' kin,
> Frae a warld o' trouble, o' sorrow, an sin.

Laing had a very positive relationship with religious life and the religious establishment as shown in the subject-matter and tone of his poems and songs and in the facts that he was invited to give advice on a collection of hymns,[6] and that it was a minister, the Reverend George Gilfillan of Dundee, who wrote the introduction to the third edition of his collection of poems and songs called *Wayside Flowers* (Laing 1857). It is not at all surprising, therefore, to find him in contact with the wife of the minister of Fearn.

Nor is it surprising that he should have collected ballads from her. There is no mention of this apart from Amelia Harris's note, but Laing's few references to the sources of the small group of ballads he collected all name ministers or their connections. Of *The Baron of Brackley* (Child 203A) he says, "I got the manuscript from Mrs. Scott, spouse to the Rev. Robert Scott, Glenbucket."[7] In the case of *Rob Roy* (Child 225K), he "blended together" two copies, commenting, "I had the first copy from Miss Harper, Kildrummy; but fearing imperfections, I made application, and by chance got another copy from the Rev. R. Scott, Glenbucket." (1823: 50) *Glenlogie* (Child 238G), as published in the anonymously edited *Ballad Minstrelsy of Scotland* (1871: 506), has the attached note: "The version which follows is based on a MS. version communicated to Mr. Buchan in a letter from Mr. Alexander Laing, dated Brechin, April 9th, 1829, and there given by him as taken down from 'the recitation of the amiable daughter of' a clergyman in the North."

---

[6] Laing's letter of advice is included in the unpaginated collection of his letters; see note 5.
[7] *The Thistle of Scotland* (1823: 50), with reference to the version published in his *Scarce Ancient Ballads* (1822: 9-12).

As noted in the passage quoted at the beginning of this appendix, Laing received material from Mrs Harris to pass on to Peter Buchan and, according to Clyne (see p. xxvi above), it was Amelia Harris who took down the words. Amelia speaks (p. 247) of "two" of the "several" ballads supplied having been published by Buchan in his *Ancient Ballads and Songs of the North of Scotland* (1828), but, since Buchan apparently amalgamated and adapted ballad versions for publication (cf. p. xxvi above), it is not clear which she is referring to. However, Buchan's manuscript "Collection of Ancient Ballads of Scotland" in the British Library includes the following two rare ballads on adjacent pages (Additional MS 29408 ff. 123-5) and it seems safe to say that they came to him from Mrs Harris. The verse numbering is editorial.

Alison.

1   My love she lives in Linco'n shire,
        I wat she's neither black nor brown,
    Her hair is like the threads o' gowd,
        Aye an' it were well kaimed down.

2   She pu'd the black mask aff her face,
        An' blinked blythely wi' her ee;
    Says, – Will ye to my wedding come,
        Or will ye bear me companie?

3   I winna to your wedding come,
        Nor will I bear you companie,
    Unless ye be the bride yoursell,
        An' me the bonny bridegroom be.

4   For me to be the bride mysell,
        An' you the bonny bridegroom be;
    Cheer up your heart Willie, she said,
        For that's the day ye'll never see.

5   Gin ye were on your saddle set,
        An' merry riding on the way;

Ye'll mind nae mair o' Alison,
  When she were dead an' laid in clay.

6   When he was on his saddle set,
  An' weary riding on the way,
He had mair mind o' Alison,
  Than he had o' the light o' day.

7   He spied a hart draw till a hare,
  And aye the hare drew near a town,
That same hart did get a hare,
  But the gentle knight got ne'er a town.

8   He lean'd his back to his saddle bow,
  And his heart did break in pieces three;
Wi' sighing said that sweet Willie,
  The pains o' luve's taen hold o' me.

9   Their wedding day it was well set,
  And a' their friends invited there,
While came a white horse and a letter,
  That stopp'd the wedding in prepare.

10   She said, if Willie he be dead,
  A wedded wife I'll never be;
Then lean'd her back to her bed stock,
  Her heart in pieces broke in three
She then was buried and bemoan'd,
  But the birds were Willie's companie.

Helen.

1   Burd Helen was her mother's dear,
  Her father's heir to be;
He was the laird o' Broughty Walls,
  And the provost o' Dundee.

2 Burd Helen she was much admired,
  By all that were round about;
 Unto Hazlen[1] she was betrothed,
  Her virgin days were out.

3 Glenhazlen was a comely youth,
  And virtuous were his friends;
 He left the schools o' bonny Dundee,
  And on to Aberdeen.

4 It fell upon a Christmas day;
  Burd Helen was left alone;
 For to keep her father's towers,
  They stand two miles from town.

5 Glenhazlen's on to Broughty Walls,
  Was thinking to win in;
 But the wind it blew, and the rain dang on,
  And wat him to the skin.

6 He was very well entertain'd
  Baith for his bed and board,
 Till a band o' men surrounded them,
  Well arm'd wi' spear and sword.

7 They hurried her along wi' them,
  Tuck'd up her maids behind;
 They threw the keys out ower the walls,
  That none the plot might find.

8 They hurried her along wi them,
  Ower mony a rock and glen;
 But all that they could say or do,
  From weeping would not refrain.

9 The hiland hills are hie, hie hills,
  The hiland hills are hie;

---

[1] The word has been revised from the way it was first written which may have begun "Hang".

They are no like the banks o' Tay,
  Or bonny town o' Dundee.

10   It fell out ance upon a day,
        They went to take the air;
      She threw hersell upon the stream,
        Against wind and despair.

11   It was sae deep, he cou'dna wide,
        Boats werna to be found;
      But he leapt in after himsell,
        And sunk down like a stone.

12   She kilted up her green claiding,
        A little below her knee;
      And never rest, nor was undrest,
        Till she reach'd again Dundee.

13   I learned this at Broughty Walls,
        At Broughty, near Dundee;
      That if water were my prison strong,
        I would swim for libertie.

Readings where MS A corresponds to Buchan

The fact that at a number of points where the Buchan and the Harris
B texts diverged, the Buchan and Harris A texts are identical or very
similar strengthens the connection between the Buchan and Harris
versions. These are:

Alison. (**4** *My luve she lives in Lincolnshire*)

  1 Buchan 2.1   She pu'd the black mask
     Harris A 2.1   She pued the black mask
     Harris B 2.1   She's pued the black mask

2	Buchan 7.1	a hart draw till a hare
	Harris A 5.1	a hart draw to a hare
	Harris B 7.1	a hart draw near a hare

3	Buchan 8.3	said that sweet Willie
	Harris A 6.3	said that sweet Willie
	Harris B 8.3	said him sweet Willie

4	Buchan 10.3	to her
	Harris A 8.1	to her
	Harris B 10.1	on her

Helen. (**14** *Burd Hellen, or Broughty Wa's*)

1	Buchan 5.2	win in
	Harris A 5.2	win in
	Harris B 5.2	get in

2	Buchan 10.1	It fell out ance upon a day
	Harris A 9.1	It fell out once upon a day
	Harris B 10.1	It fell out once upon a time

3	Buchan 10.4	Against wind and despair
	Harris A 9.4	Against wind and despair
	Harris B 10.4	Between wind an' despair

4	Buchan 11.1	It was sae deep
	Harris A 10.1	It was sae deep
	Harris B 11.1	The stream was deep

5	Buchan 13.3	my prison strong
	Harris A 13.3	my prison strong
	Harris B 13.3	my prison walls

This pattern of variation, of course, suggests retention of the older form up to 1859 and revisions being made later.

Readings where MS B corresponds to Buchan

There is another clearly marked pattern according to which the A text varies from the other two, showing the older form of c. 1829 being recaptured in 1872 rather than the form set down in 1859, the 1859 words not becoming established, and perhaps, of course, in some cases being mere slips in setting down.

Alison.

1	Buchan 1.2	I wat
	Harris A 1.2	An' I wat
	Harris B1.2	I wat
2	Buchan	vs 5-6
	Harris A	no equivalent verses
	Harris B	vs 5-6
3	Buchan 10.3	her back
	Harris A 8.1	her head
	Harris B 10.1	her back

Helen.

1	Buchan 1.1	mother's
	Harris A 1.1	mother
	Harris B 1.1	mother's
2	Buchan 1.3	Broughty Walls
	Harris A 1.3	Broughty halls
	Harris B 1.3	Brochty Walls
3	Buchan 1.4	And the provost o' Dundee
	Harris A 1.4	O' Broughty ne'ar Dundee
	Harris B 1.4	An' Provost of Dundee [erased reading]

4	Buchan 3.4	And on
	Harris A 3.4	And he's on
	Harris B 3.4	An' on

5	Buchan 8.3	But all that they
	Harris A 8.3	And a' that he
	Harris B 8.3	But a' that they

6	Buchan 9.3	o' Tay
	Harris A 12.3	o' the Tay
	Harris B 12.3	o' Tay

7	Buchan 11.4	And sunk
	Harris A 10.4	And he sank
	Harris B 11.4	An' sank

8	Buchan 12.3	And never
	Harris A 11.3	And she never
	Harris B 13.3	An' never

Readings where MSS A and B correspond

Most of the variations take the form of Harris A and B (both derived from Amelia Harris) differing from the Buchan form (derived from Mrs Harris), suggesting that there was movement away from the source by 1859 and that divergences from it have been retained. There is, however, the possibility of the Buchan text having been adapted by Alexander Laing (who probably transmitted it to Buchan) or by Buchan himself and this point will be discussed below in relation to the differences affecting more than a single line. In the following list of small differences the two possibilities have to be kept in mind. The distinctive Buchan reading is given first and the two identical or similar Harris readings are given in brackets with MS A first in each case.

Alison.

1.3 Her hair (But her hair, But her hair); 2.1 aff her face (oer her face, owre her face); 2.2 blythely (gayly, gaily); 2.3 Says, – Will ye (Oh will you, Oh! will you); 2.4 Or (And, An'); companie (gude companie, gude companie); 3.2 companie (gude companie, gude companie); 3.4 bridegroom be (bridgroom to be, bridegroom to be); 4.2 be (to be, to be); 4.3 Willie (sweet Willie, sweet Willie); 5.2 merry (A *lacking*, B gaily); 5.3 Ye'll mind nae mair (A *lacking*, B You'll hae nae mair mind); 5.4 When (A *lacking*, B Than); 6.2 weary (A *lacking*, B slowly); 7.1 spied (saw, saw); 7.3 That (And that, An' that), 8.1 his back to (him o'er, him owre); 8.4 luve's taen (love hae tane, luve hae ta'en); 9.1-2 *2 lines not in A or B*; 9.3 = Harris 9.1 While (There, There); 9.4 = Harris 9.2 in prepare (speedilie, speidilie); 10.1-2 *2 lines not in A or B* ; 10.3 = Harris 10.1 Then (She, She); bed stock (bed side, bedside); 10.4 = Harris 10.2 Her (And her, An' her); in pieces broke (did brak in pieces, did brak in pieces); 10.5 = Harris 10.3 She then (She, She).

Helen.

2.3 Unto Hazlen (But to Hunglen, But to Hunglen); 3.2 were his (his, his); 4.1 fell upon a Christmas day (fell out once upon a time, fell oot once upon a time); 4.3 For (A' for, All for); 5.1 Glenhazlen's on to Broughty Walls (Glen Slagen [?] he cam ridin' by, Glenhazlen he cam ridin' bye); 5.2 Was thinking (A' thinkin', An' thinkin); 7.1 hurried (heysed, hiesèd); 7.2 Tuck'd [probably copying error for Lock'd] (Locked, Locked); 7.3 They threw (And flang, An' flang); 8.1 hurried (heysed, hiesèd); 8.4 From weeping (To weep she, To weep she); 9.3/12.3 They are no like the banks (Their no like the pleasant banks/ They're no like the pleasant banks); 9.4/12.4 Or (Nor, Nor); 10.2 went (went out, went out); 10.3 upon (in to, in-to); 11.3 But he (So he, So he); after himsell (after her himsel, after her himsel); 14.4 would (could, could).

In Harris B, a "Highland hills" verse occurs twice, in a "departure" form before the leap into the stream (verse 9) and in a "return" form after the leap (verse 12). Harris A has only the return form at the return point (verse 12), while Buchan has only the following return form at the departure point (verse 9):

The hiland hills are hie, hie hills,
  The hiland hills are hie,
They are no like the banks o' Tay,
  Or bonny town o' Dundee.

There was evidently some uncertainty about the placing of this partially recurrent verse, and this uncertainty is illustrated also by the difference in order between the return "Highland hills" verse and the verse beginning "She kilted up" in the two Harris MSS texts. There is no indication that the treatment of this element in the Buchan text is untraditional here though it does not directly match with either Harris text. The matter is more problematic in the case of *Alison*, where it is quite possible that the Buchan text contains material composed by either Buchan or Laing to supply the lacuna in verse 9 which is now known to be a feature of Harris A as well as Harris B, and also the extra two lines at the opening of verse 10 which are not present in A or B.

APPENDIX C

CHILD'S USE OF MS B IN
THE ENGLISH AND SCOTTISH POPULAR BALLADS

This appendix lists the ballads in the order in which they occur in Child's edition, and indicates the use that Child made of MS B. The numbers of the ballads in this edition are shown in bold print. Where Child's reading differs from that of the present edition, his reading is given, followed by the reading of this edition in brackets. Child's emendations are included in the notes.

Child 4 *Lady Isabel and the Elf-Knight* Bd (**23**)
Although Child does not give this fragment a separate letter he prints it in full in his notes (l.60-1). 1.1 brown (broun); 4.1 and (an').

Child 10 *The Twa Sisters,* music only (**55**)

Child 11 *The Cruel Brother* C, with music (**5**)
4.3 brither (brother); 15.3 our (oor); 18.1 ye (you).

Child 20 *The Cruel Mother* Ja, with music (**12**)
4.1 O (Oh); 5.1 O (Oh); 5.3 an (&); 6.1 O (Oh); 7.1 O (Oh); 9.1 Ye (You); 9.3 i (in); 10.1 i (in).

Child 46 *Captain Wedderburn's Courtship* Be, with music (**11**)
Child gives only variants from the Kinloch version. 1.2 out (oot).

Child 47 *Proud Lady Margaret* D, with music (**3**)
1.3 lady (ladie); 3.1 lady (ladie); 8.1 hie (high); 13.1 bracht (brocht); 14.3 bracht (brocht).

Child 53 *Young Beichan*, music only (**59**)

Child 58 *Sir Patrick Spens* J, with music (**1**)
5.1 O (Oh); 11.3 When (Whan); 12.3 When (Whan), wind (winds); 13.1 O (Oh); 14.1 O (Oh); 19.1 O (Oh), oor (our); 21.4 Sir Patrick Spens (Sir Patrick); 23.1 O (Oh).

Child 61 *Sir Cawline* appendix, with music (**2**)
6.2 Very (Verie); 11.2 out (oot); 12.2 An (I an'); 15.2 flee (free).

Child 63 *Child Waters* E, with music (**18**)
9.3 could (culd); 11.1 learnt in (learnt it in); 11.4 weel (well); 13.4 hame (home); 16.3 Erse (Ershe); 20.3 travisse (travis); 23.2 shall (sall).

Child 68 *Young Hunting* C, with music (**7**)
6.1 saddle-bow (saidle bow); 9.2 an (&); 16.3 is it (it is).

Child 75 *Lord Lovel* G (**35**)
2.1 O (Oh), goin (gaen); 6.1 not (na); 7.1 an (and); 7.2 Edenborrow (Edinborrow).

Child 77 *Sweet William's Ghost*, music only (**54**)

Child 84 *Bonny Barbara Allan*, music only (**56**)

Child 87 *Prince Robert* D (**36**)

Child 89 *Fause Foodrage* C, with music (**29**)
1.2 And (An'); three (thrie); 1.4 gay (gey); 2.3 o (a).

Child 93 *Lamkin* V (**32**)

Child 98 *Brown Adam* B, with music (**25**)

Child 106 *The Famous Flower of Serving-Men*, music only (**17**)
Child does not print the Harris fragment, but mentions it in his headnote, saying that it is derived from the broadside he prints.

Child 114 *Johnnie Cock* G and L, with music (**13**)
G: 1.1 Brad (Brod). L: note 5 cat (cut).

Child 164 *King Henry Fifth's Conquest of France*, music only (**31**)
Child makes no mention of the Harris text.

Child 169 *Johnie Armstrong*, music only (**10**)
Child makes no mention of the Harris text.

Child 173 *Mary Hamilton* J, with music (**16**)
1.2 proud, proud (proud); 3.2 kamis (kaims); 4.4 seek (sick).

Child 182 *The Laird o Logie* D, with music (**6**)
3.2 Wringin (Wringing); 6.1 house (houses); 9.4 let (set); 10.2 cald (culd).

Child 191 *Hughie Grame* G (**24**)

Child 225 *Rob Roy* [L] (**26**)
This fragment occurs in "Additions and Corrections" at 4.523. It has no letter but the version before it is lettered K.

Child 234 *Charlie MacPherson* A (**15**)
3.1 Whan (When); 7.1 Whan (When); 8.2 glancet (glancit).

Child 235 *The Earl of Aboyne* E, with music (**30**)

Child 238 *Glenlogie, or, Jean o Bethelnie* D (**8**)

Child 246 *Redesdale and Wise William* B (**9**)
5.2 nicht, *note, perhaps* "necht" (nicht); 6.2 licht, *note, perhaps* "leiht" (licht); 12.3 Sa (Sae); 16.1 bowr (bour); 17.2 bour (bowr).

Child 252 *The Kitchie-Boy* D (**20**)

Child 256 *Alison and Willie* A, with music (**4**)
1.2 neither (niether); 1.3 thread (threads); 2.3 O, *note,* Oh (Oh); 7.4 neer (neir).

Child 258 *Broughty Wa's* B, with music (**14**)
Child prints only the variants from Peter Buchan's version taken from the Harvard copy of British Library Additional MSS 29408-9 which is Houghton Library MS 25241.10*. For Buchan's text, see Appendix B. 4.4 ten (two).

Child 277 *The Wife Wrapt in Wether's Skin* B (**21**)
2.1, 3.1, 4.1 neither (niether); 6.1 gaun (gane); 6.3 blaik (black).

GLOSSARY

This glossary is supplied as an aid to comprehension of words in the songs that might present difficulty; for further information, the reader is referred to *The Concise Scots Dictionary* ed. Mairi Robinson (Aberdeen 1985) and *The Scottish National Dictionary* ed. William Grant and David D. Murison (Edinburgh 1931-75).

a', *adj,* all, 1A 19.3; 1B 21.3; 2A 1.2, 1.4; 2B 1.2 etc.

a', *adv*, all, 3A 11.4; 3B 11.4; 6B 7.4, 8.4 etc.

abe, abee, a-bee, *v*, be, 1A 5.4; 1B 5.4; 6A 4.2; 6B 4.2; 8A 8.2 etc.

aboon, aboun, *adv*, above, on top of, 1A 18.4; 1B 19.4; 7B 19.3; 9A 18.3; 9B 18.3 etc.

ace, *adj*, ash, fireside, 33 note

adoon, adown, *adv*, down, 12A 1.4, 2.4, 3.4; 12B 1.4, 2.4, 3.4 etc.

ae, *adj*, one, only, single, 3A 10.1, 11.1; 3B 10.1, 11.1; 7A 21.4; 7B 21.4 etc.

afore, *conj*, before, 1A 21.3, 22.3, 23.3; 1B 23.3, 24.3 etc.

ahint, *prep,* behind, 40 3.2; 51 6.1, 17.3

alake, *interj*, alas, 1A 7.2; 1B 8.3

amrie, *n*, cupboard, 39 6.2

ance, *adv*, once, 25B 3.1

ane, *adj*, one, 2A 1.2; 2B 1.2; 12A 2.1, 5.1; 12B 2.1, 5.1 etc.

aneath, *prep*, beneath, 13B 6.4

anither, *pron*, each other, 18A 16.3; 18B 16.3

asken, askin, *n*, request, 18A 25.1, 26.1, 27.1; 18B 22.1, 23.1, 24.1 etc.; **askens, asken's,** *pl*, 6A 5.2, 5.3; 6B 5.2, 5.3

atween, *prep*, between, 9A 1.3; 9B 1.3, 15.4; 13A 2.2; 13B 5.2 etc.

aucht, *adj*, eight, 8A 1.1, 2.1; 8B 1.1, 2.1; 10A 1.4 etc

ava, *adv phr*, at all, 41 5.1

awa, *adv*, away, 3B 4.2, 8.2; 8A 6.4; 8B 7.4 etc.

aye, *adv*, always, continually, 4A 5.2; 4B 7.2; 5A 1.4, 2.4; 5 B 1.4, 2.4 etc.

aye, *interj*, yes, 2A 2.2; 2B 2.2; 4A 1.4; B 1.4; 11B 2.2 etc.

aye, for **a'**, *adv,* all, 6A 3.4, 7.4, 9.4; 6B 3.4

baken, *adj*, baked, 2A 3.3; 2B 3.3; 13A 4.1; 13B 4.1

ben, *adv*, in or to the inner part of the house, 39 7.2; 41 12.4; **ther ben,** within there 41 12.4; 46 1.2

benison, *n*, blessing, 13A 4.3; 13B 4.3

bide, *v*, remain, stay, 1A 6.3; 1B 7.3; 3A 4.4, 5.1; 3B 4.4, 5.1 etc.

biggit, *v pt*, built, 20B 4.1

birlin, birl'in, birlin', *v pres p*, carousing, 1A 1.2; 1B 1.2; 9A 1.2; 9B1.2; 18A 20.2; 18B 17.2

bit, *adj*, little, 38 5.2; 39 1.4

bittie, *n*, little bit, 39 1.1, 2.1

blad, *n*, violent thrust, 39 4.4

bletherin, *adj*, blubbering, 38 11.4

blink, *n*, look, glance, 9A 3.4, 4.4; 9B 3.4, 4.4

blinkèd, blinkit, *v pt*, looked, 4A 2.2; 4B 2.2; 34 1.2

blinkin, *adj*, cheating, 41 7.1

blues, *n*, blue clothes, possibly a uniform, 39 3.1

boddam, *n*, bottom, 1B 17.4

bodie, *n*, person, being, 7A 1.4; 7B 1.4; 38 8.2

bogles, *n pl*, ugly phantoms, usually ill-dispositioned, 41 2.1

bonnie, *adj*, good-looking, 1A 2.1, 12.1, 13.1; 1B 2.1, 13.1, 14.1 etc.; **bonniest,** *superl*, 13A 10.3; 13B 10.3; 16A 10.3; 16B 10.3

bound, boun, *adj*, prepared, ready, swollen, 2A 12.2; 2B 12.2; 3A 3.2, 4.2; 3B 3.2, 4.2 etc.

bour, bowr, *n*, bower, dwelling, lady's private apartment, 1A 15.3; 1B 16.3; 2A 5.3; 2B 5.3; 17A 2.1 etc.; **bours,** *pl*, 16A 1.3

bourswoman, *n*, bower-woman, waiting-woman, 7A 7.1, 23.1, 24.1; 7B 7.1, 24.1, 25.1

bran, bran', *n*, grain husks, 18A 3.2, 4.2; 18B 5.2, 6.2

brand, *n*, sword, 2A 11.2, 11.3

braw, *adj*, fine-looking, fine, 15A 1.1; 15B 1.1; 37 2.4, 2.5 etc.

brawly, *adv*, well, 38 6.2

bree, brie, *n*, brow, forehead, 9A 3.2, 4.2, 18.3; 9B 3.2, 4.2, 18.3

brig, *n*, bridge, 22A 4.4; 22B 4.4; 36 8.1, 9.1

broad, *adj*; **broad letter,** letter on a broad sheet or a long letter, 1A 3.1; 1B 3.1; 9A 5.1; 9B 5.1; 10B 2.1

brunt, *v pt*, burnt, 6A 2.1; 6B 2.1

buckies, *n pl*, whelks, wild-rose hips, 48 1.1, 1.2

buckles, *v pres*, joins in marriage, 38 9.3

burd, *n*, lady, 14A 1.1, 2.1, 4.2; 14B 1.1, 2.1, 4.2 etc.

but, *prep*, without, 3B 3.4; **bot an',** besides, as well as, and also, 13B 2.2

butt, *prep*; **butt the hoose,** in the outer rooms of the house, 46 1.1

bye, *adj*, side, 18A 20.3; 18B 17.3; **in bye,** from the outside to the inside, 51 16.1

byres, *n pl*, cow-sheds, 51 3.2

ca'd, ca'ed, *v pp*, pushed, 11A 8.4, 14.4; 11B 7.4, 11.4

caird, *v*, card, prepare wool for spinning by combing, 21A 4.1, 11.1; 21B 3.1, 11.1

cannel, *adj,* candle, 7B 3.2, 4.2

cannels, *n pl,* 7B 19.4, 20.4

canny, *adj*, wise, 51 4.3

canty, *adj*, lively, 38 5.2

catched, *v pt*, caught, 34 1.4, 2.4

caups, *n pl,* cups, bowls, 39 6.3

chappit, *v pt*, knocked, 51 8.1

chiel, *n*, young man, 38 11.3

clied, *v*, clothe, 12B 6.3, 7.3; **clead,** *pp*, 30 7.3

clieden, cleidin', cleiden, cleadin', cleading, *n*, clothing, 14A 11.1; 14B 13.1; 18A 7.3; 18B 7.3; 23A 4.3

close, *n*, passageway, 5A 14.1; 5B 14.1

close, *v pp*, closed, 41 1.3

cloutie, *n*, rag, 33 note

cloutit, *v pp*, patched, 33 note

coft, *v pp*; **Dear Coft, Dear-Coft,** dearly bought, 2A 18.4; 2B 18.4

coll, cole, *n*, haycock, 22A 1.2; 22B 1.2

coost, *v pt*, threw, cast off, 29A 1.3; 29B 1.3; 36 9.2

corse, *n*, cross, market-cross, town-cross, 37 2.2

crab tree, *n*, wild fruit tree, 27 2.1

crack, *n*, moment, 30 6.3

crap, *v pt*, crept, 40 3.2

criesh, *v*, grease, 40 2.3

crouse, *adj*, confident, 38 2.3

culd, cald, *v pt*, could, 6B 10.2; 18B 9.3, 11.3 etc.

culverine, *n*, long cannon, 52 1.6

cummers, *n pl*, women, female acquaintances, 37 1.7, 2.7, 3.7 etc.

cut, *n*, piece, 13B note

daurna, *v neg*, dare not, 2A 7.4; 2B 7.4; 21A 8.1; 21B 8.1; 36 1.2

deal, *v*, distribute, 35 9.1, 9.4, 10.1 etc.; **dealt,** *pt*, 35 11.1, 11.4, 12.1 etc.

dee, *v*, die, 2A 2.4, 6.2; 2B 2.4, 6.2; 6A 3.4; 6B 3.4 etc.

dee, *v*, do, 9A 2.4, 16.2; 9B 2.4, 16.2

deed, *adv*, indeed, 38 3.1; 41 2.3

degree, *n*, rank, 6A 12.2; 6B 12.2; 31 6.2, 8.2 etc

deid, *n*, death, 29B 4.4

dichted, *v pt*, wiped, 38 10.3

dine, *n*, dinner, 8A 2.2; 8B 2.2

ding, *v*, strike, knock, 2A 17.4; 2B 17.4; 13A 2.4; 13B 5.4; 37 2.2; **dung,** *pp*, 2A 17.2; 2B 17.2; **dang on,** fell heavily and continuously, 14A 5.3; 14B 5.3

dinna, *v neg*, do not, does not, 2A 1.4; 2B 1.4; 3A 2.1, 3.1; 3B 2.1, 3.1; 12A 10.3; 12B 10.3 etc.

dish-cloot, *v*, dish-cloth, 38 11.1

divot, *n*, thin piece of turf, 50 note

dominie, *n*; **whittlegait dominie,** teacher receiving payment in the form of meals taken at the homes of the scholars, 19B note

doo, *n*, dove, 38 5.1

douce, *adj*, pleasant, gentle, lovable, 41 10.3

dowie, *adj*, doleful, sad, 7A 20.3, 21.3; 7B 21.3, 22.3; 16A 7.1; 16B 7.1 etc.

drie, *v*, suffer, endure, 7A 24.4; 7B 25.4

dried, *v*; **drieds me,** makes me afraid, 7A 17.3; 7B 17.3

driving, drivin, *v pres p*, propelling, riding hard on horseback, 1A 9.4, 11.4, 22.4; 1B 10.4, 12.4, 24.4

dyke, *n*, wall, 41 3.2

dykeside, *n*, ground alongside a wall, 15A 2.1, 6.1; 15B 2.1, 6.1

ee, ee', *n*, eye, 1A 4.4, 6.2, 15.2; 1B 4.4, 16.2 etc.; **een,** *pl*, 39 5.3, 7.4; 51 15.2

eldern, *adj*, elderly, 2A 2.1; 2B 2.1

elson, *n*, shoemaker's awl, 50 note

eneuch, *adj*, enough, 2B 13.3

Erse, Ershe, *n*, Gaelic, 18A 16.3; 18B 16.3

even, *adv*, steadily, straight, 2A 2.2, 14.2, 16.2; 2B 2.2, 14.2, 16.2

even, ee'n, *n*, evening, 2A 12.1; 2B 12.1; 15A 1.2; 15B 1.2; 51 3.4

ever, *adv*, always, 1A 7.3; 1B 8.3

faddoms, *n*, fathoms, 1B 21.2

faem, *n;* **see faem,** sea foam, 23B 2.4

fain, *adv*, gladly, 7A 16.4; 7B 16.4; 18A 20.4; 18B 17.4

fair, *n*; **fair fa',** good fortune befall, good luck to, 15A 1.4, 5.4; 15B 1.4, 5.4

fand, *v pt*, found, 13B note; 36 10.2

farer, *comp adj,* farther, 23A 3.4; 23B 4.4

fash, *n*, bother, annoyance, 51 3.3

fash, *v*, bother, trouble, 38 3.3

faun, *v pp*, fallen, 20B 1.3

fause, *adj*, false, 12A 5.1; 12B 5.1, 7.1; 23A 6.1; 23B 6.1 etc.

faut, *n*, fault, 41 7.2

feal, *n*, turf used as building material, 50 note

feared, *adj*, afraid, 40 2.2

fee, *n*, wealth, money, 29A 2.2; 29B 2.2; 36 6.2, 7.2

fexèd, *v pt*, fixed, 39   5.3

firsten, first an, first an', first and, *adj*, first, 1A 4.1; 1B 4.1; 7A
20.1; 7B 21.1; 13A 7.1, 11.1; 13B 7.1 etc.

flang, *v pt*, flung, threw, 7A 9.4, 23.4; 7B 9.4, 24.4; 13A 11.3; 13B
11.3 etc.

fleyed, *v*, frightened, scared, 51 13.1

flingstrings, *n*, sulks, 37 1.2

forlorn, *pp*, destroyed, 7A 17.4; 7B 17.4

forn, *v pp*, provided for, especially with food and drink, 1A 8.2; 1B
6.2, 9.2

fou, *adj*, drunk, 50 1.4

frae, *prep*, from, 2A 13.4; 2B 8.3, 13.4; 5A 3.1; 5B 3.1 etc.

free, *adj*, unattached, lacking in goods, valuable, 9A 19.4; 9B 19.4;
20A 12.4; 20B 10.4; *adv*, freely, 2A 15.2; 2B 15.2; 20A 12.4;
20B 10.4

fu, fu', *adv*, very, extremely, 7A 10.2; 7B 10.2; 15A 8.2

fule, *n*, fool, simpleton, 51 13.2

ga', *n*, gall, 11A 7.2, 11.2; 11B 6.2, 10.2

gae, ge, *v*, go, 1A 12.3; 2B 4.4; 6A 8.3 etc.; **gaes,** *pres,* 3A 6.1,
6.3, 7.1; 3B 6.1, 6.3, 7.1 etc.; **gaen,** *pres p*, 35 2.1; 39 6.2; 51
9.1; **gaed,** *pt*, 11A 1.2; 11B 1.2; 15A 1.2, 2.4; 15B 2.4 etc.;
gane, gaen, *pp*, 1A 14.1; 1B 15.1; 3B 3.3; 6A 12.4; 6B 12.4
etc.

gainst, *prep*, against, in time for, in, 35 9.3, 10.3, 11.3 etc.

gairies, *n pl*, crags, black and yellow striped wild bees, striped cows,
48 1.1

gang, gieng, *v*, go, 1A 13.3; 2A 3.4, 4.4; 2B 3.4

gar, *v*, make, 37 1.1, 2.1, 3.1 etc.

gay, gey, *adj*, fine, pretty, 3A 3.1; 3B 3.1; 5A 1.2; 5B 1.2; 11A 8.3;
11B 7.3 etc.

gentle, *adj*, noble, 3A 2.1; 3B 2.1; 4A 5.4; 4B 7.4; 44 9.1; **gentlest,**
superl, 18A 18.3, 19.3

gie, *v*, give, ; 2B 9.3; 6A 5.2, 13.2; 6B 5.2, 13.2 etc.; **gied,** for **gie't,**
give it, 22A 2.3, 3.3; **gie's,** give me, 13 note; **gae,** *pt*, 1A 4.2;
1B 4.2; 2A 7.2, 10.1; 2B 7.2, 10.1 etc.; **gie leave,** *v*, let go,
abandon, 3A 13.4; 3B 13.4

gif, *conj*, if, 1B 3.4; 12B 6.1

gin, *conj,* if, 4B 5.1; 30 5.3; 37 1.3 etc.

girns, *v pres*, complains peevishly, 38 9.2

223

glack, *n*, hollow, ravine, confined place, 10A 13.1; 10B 13.1

glancèd, glancit, *v pt*, gleamed, 15A 8.2; 15B 8.2

glass, *n*, mirror, 1A 17.2; 1B 18.2

gled, *n*, kite, buzzard, hawk, 22A 1.3; 22B 1.3

glue, gloe, *n*, glove, 6A 9.2, 11.4; 6B 8.4, 9.2, 11.4 etc.

glush, *n*, mud, 51 7.3

goup, *v*, gape, 39 5.2

gowd, gow'd, goud, *n*, gold, 2A 16.4; 2B 16.4; 3A 13.2; 3B 13.2; 4A 1.3; 4B 1.3 etc.

greet, *v*, weep; **greetin, greitin,** *pres p*, 16A 3.4; 16B 3.4; **grat,** *pp*, 38 10.3

gude, *adj*, good, 1A 2.3, 8.4; 1B 2.3, 6.4, 9.4 etc.

gudesake, *n*, God's sake, 12B 12.3

gudeson, gude son, *n*, son-in-law, 15A 3.4; 15B 3.4

hae, *v*, have, 1A 5.2, 5.3, 5.4; 1B 5.3 etc; **haen, hain,** *pp*, 18A 20.4; 18B 17.4

hand write, *n*, handwriting, 6A 9.1, 11.3; 6B 8.3, 9.1, 11.3

hangit, *v pt*, hanged, 12A 2.3, 6.3

hankit, *v pt*, tied tightly with a loop, constricted, 12B 2.3, 8.3

haud, had, *v*, travel in a certain direction, hold, keep, 1A 1.5; 2A 17.1; 2B 17.1; 6A 4.1; 6B 4.1 etc.

haugh, *n*, piece of flat land, usually beside a river, 13B 10.1; **haughs,** *pl*, 13A 10.1

hause bone, hasebane, *n*, collar bone, 7A 15.3; 7B 15.3

here, *v*, probably misunderstanding of **hear,** 41 1.1, 1.3

heysed, hiesèd, *v pt,* carried, hurried, hustled off, 14A 7.1, 8.1; 14B 7.1, 8.1

hie, *adv*, high; 1A 1.1, 14.2; 1B 1.1, 15.2; 14B 9.2 etc.

hie, *v*, travel quickly, hasten, come quickly, 1B 1.5; **hieing, hiean, hiching,** *pres p*, 1A 23.4; 1B 23. 4; 7A 2.4; 7B 2.4

hieland, *adj*, Highland, 14B 9.1, 9.2; 15A 1.1; 15B 1.1

hielands, Hielands, *n pl*, Highlands, 18A 1.3, 2.3, 16.1; 18B 1.3, 2.3, 16.1 etc

him, *redundant pron*, that, 2A 1.3, 12.3; 2B 1.3, 12.3; 7A 9.4; 7B 9.4 etc.

hindy, *adj*, courteous, gentle, kindly, 3A 5.1, 9.1; 3B 5.1, 9.1

hollin, *n*, holly, 21A 1.2, 2.2, 3.2; 21B 1.2, 2.2, 3.2 etc.

i, i', *prep*, in, 12B 11.3, 12.1; 23B 2.4 etc.

I, for **aye,** *interj*, yes, 2A 12.2; 2B 12.2

ilka, *adj*, every, each, 1A 14.3; 13B note; 28A 3.1 etc.

into, intil, *prep*, in, 1A 21.2; 1B 22.2, 23.2; 2A 14.4; 2B 14.4 etc.

Ise, *pron, v fut,* I shall, I'll, 38 3.1, 6.4

it, *pron* (as *indefinite demonstrative*), there, 1B 2.1, 7.1, 18.1 etc.

jaws, *n,* waves, 1A 9.3, 10.3, 11.3; 1B 10.3, 11.3, 12.3

kaim, *n,* comb, 16A 3.2; **kaims,** *pl,* 16B 3.2

kaim, *v,* comb, 38 2.1; **kaimed, kaimèd,** *pt,* 4A 1.4; 4B 1.4; 20A 8.2; 20B 6.2

keep, *v,* guard, 14A 4.3; 14B 4.3; **keepit,** *pt,* maintained, protected, 10A 1.4; 10B 1.4, 10.3; **in keepin, keepin',** in (their) care, 15A 1.4; 15B 1.4

kemp, *v,* strive to win the contest, 47 1.1

ken, *v,* know, 16A 9.1; 16B 9.1; 20B   6.3; 32 1.4 etc.; **kent, kenned,** *pt, pp,* 10B 10.1; 15A 7.2; 15B 7.2; 20A 8.3; 20B 8.3 etc.

kene, *adj,* keen, sharp, 13B 2.2

keppit, *v pt,* caught, 7A 6.3; 7B 6.3

kevils, *n,* pieces of wood for casting lots, 29A 1.3; 29B 1.3

kilted, *v pt,* tucked, 14A 11.1; 14B 13.1; 18A 7.3; 18B 7.3

kintrie, *n,* country, 55 1.3

kirk, *n,* church, 3B 13.1, 14.1; 22B 5.3 etc.

kirkin', kirken, *n,* churching, a mother's first attendance at church after the birth of a child, 18A 29.3; 18B 26.3

kirkyard, kirkyaird, *n,* churchyard, 3A 10.3, 13.3, 14.3; 3B 10.3, 13.3, 14.3 etc.

kitchie, *adj,* kitchen, 20B 1.3

knock, *n,* clock, 39 6.2

knowe, *n,* knoll, little hill, 38 10.2; **knowes,** *pl,* 34 2.2

lad, *n,* young man, 15A 1.1; 15B 1.1; 41 2.4, 5.4

laddie, *n,* young man, 58 1.5

laid, *v pt,* brought down, reduced, 13A 7.4; 13B 7.4

laigh heele'd, *adj,* low-heeled, 1A 18.2

laird, *n,* landowner, 6A 1.4, 5.4, 10.4; 6B 1.4, 5.4, 10.4 etc.

laith, *adj,* loath, unwilling, reluctant, 1A 18.1; 1B 19.1; 15A 8.3; 15B 8.3; 28A 4.4

Lammas, *n,* 1 August, 7A 16.1; 7B 16.1; 19A 1.1; 19B 1.1

landen, *n,* landing, 1B 17.3

lane, *adj;* **her lane,** by herself, 36 10.2; **my lane,** by myself, 41 4.4

lap, *v pt,* leapt, 51 11.1

lass, *n,* young woman, 26A 1.3; 38 9.3; 41 5.4 etc.; **lasses,** *pl,* 15B note on air; 41 4.3, 5.3

lassie, *n,* young woman, 27A 1.3; 41 10.3; 45 1.1 etc.

lat, *v,* let, 6A 4.2, 8.2; 6B 4.2, 8.2, 8.6 etc.; **latten,** *pp,* 1A 5.4; 1B 5.4; 38 8.4

lauchter, *n,* laugh, 1A 4.2; 1B 4.2; 9A 6.2; 9B 6.2

lawn, *n,* fine linen, 7A 22.2; 7B 23.2

league, *n,* unit of distance, around three miles, 1A 9.1, 9.2, 10.1; 1B 10.1, 10.2, 11.1 etc.

lealer, *compar adj,* truer, 25B 1.1

lee, le, *adj,* blessed, eerie , 25A 2.4; 25B 3.4

leed, lied, *n,* verbal lore, 3A 5.3, 9.3; 3B 5.3, 9.3

lichted, lichtit, *v pt,* dismounted, landed, 18A 16.2; 18B16.2; 39 4.4

lien, *v pp,* lain, 16B 2.3

Lincoln green, Lincoln-green, *n,* green cloth made in Lincoln, 13A 5.4, 13B 2.4

line, *n,* row of ships in battle order, 52 1.6

linn, *n,* pool below a waterfall, 7A 9.3; 7B 9.3

lippie, *n,* a dry measure, 1/4 of a Scots peck, nearly a kilogram, 28A 3.2

little, *adj,* humble, lowly, inferior, 18A 26.4, 28.4; 18B 23.4, 25.4

loan, *n,* grassland, strip of grass running though arable land, 2A 14.2, 16.2; 2B 14.2, 16.2

loe, *v,* love, 41 9.2; **loed, lo'ed,** *pt,* 18A 3.4, 4.4, 5.4; 18B 3.4, 4.4, 5.4

loun, loon, *n,* young man, fellow, 6A 13.3; 6B 13.3; 51 14.4

loup, *v,* leap, jump, 18A 11.4; 18B 10.4; 37 4.2

Lowrie, *n,* a name given to the fox, 40 2.1, 4.1

luik, *v,* look, 1B 13.4, 14.4; **luikin,** *pres p,* 3B 1.4; 6B 10.2; 10B 14.2; **luikit, luiket, luekit,** *pt,* 1A 4.1; 1B 4.1; 9A 6.1; 9B 6.1; 13B 6.1 etc.

lum, *n,* chimney, 41 1.3, 12.2

lyin in, time of giving birth, 40 1.4, 4.4

make, *n,* equal, match, 8A 10.2; 8B 8.2

mammy, mammie, *n,* midwife, 51 8.1, 10.1, 12.3 etc.

Marie, *n,* lady-in-waiting, 6A 2.4; 6B 2.4; 16A 10.4; 36 3.1; **maries, Maries, Mairie's,** *pl,* 2A 4.3; 2B 4.3; 16A 8.1, 10.1; 16B 8.1, 10.1

marrow, *n,* partner in marriage, 5A 5.3; 5B 5.3

mast, *v,* must, 15A 4.3

mat, *v,* may, 9A 19.2; 29B 4.4

maun, *v,* must, 2A 3.4; 2B 3.4; 3A 14.4; 7A 18.2; 7B 19.2 etc.

mavis, *n,* song-thrush, 45 2.2

meat, *n*, food, 6A 6.3; 6B 6.3; 10A 7.3; 10B 7.3; 18A 23.2; 18B 20.2 etc.

mill, *n*, snuff-box, 38 4.3; 39 3.3

mind, *n*, recollection, thought, 4B 5.3, 6.3

mind, *v*, take care of, 51 16.1

Monnanday, Monnonday, *n*, Monday, 1A 20.2; 1B 20.2

morn, *n*; **the morn,** tomorrow, 1A 8.4; 1B 6.4, 9.4; 6B 6.3 etc.

muckle, mickle, *adj*, large, extensive, much, 1A 5.3; 1B 5.3; 9A 18.3; 9B 18.3; 20A 1.2; 20B 1.2 etc.

muir, *n*, moor, 29A 1.1, 2.1, 2.2; 29B 1.1, 2.1, 2.2 etc.

mumping, *v pres p*, nibbling, 34 2.3

na, *adv*, no, 11A 4.4, 7.4, 9.4; 11B 6.4, 8.4, 10.4 etc.

na, no, *adv*, not, 2A 4.2; 2B 4.2; 7A 17.1, 20.3; 7B 17.1 etc.

nae, *adj*, no, 2A 6.4, 17.4; 2B 6.4, 17.4; 4B 5.3 etc.

naur, *prep*, near, 2A 15.1; 2B 15.1

neb, nib, *n*, beak, 22A 3.1; 22B 2.1

nexten, next an, next and, *adj*, next, 7A 22.1; 7B 21.1; 13A 7.3; 13B 7.3

nice, *adj*, fastidious, particular, 41 6.2, 11.1

nicht, *n*; **the nicht,** tonight, 16A 8.2; 16B 8.2, 10.2

niest, *adj*, next, 5B 5.1, 8.1; 41 12.1

noo, nou, *adv*, now, 2B 17.3; 6B 4.1; 18A 23.1 etc.

nookie, *n*, corner, 33 note

och, *interj*, alas, 1A 19.1; 1B 21.1

or, *conj*, before, 1A 18.3; 2A 15.1; 40 2.4

ot, for **o't,** of it, 49 1.1, 1.2

outowre, out owre, *prep*, right over, 12B 3.1; 14A 7.3; 14B 7.3; 38 10.2

owre, *adv*, over, overly, excessively, 18A 1.4, 2.4, 26.4; 18B 1.4, 2.4, 23.4 etc.

owre, ower, *prep*, over, across, 1A 1.5, 19.1; 1B 1.5, 21.1; 2A 1.1; 2B 1.1 etc.

oxter, *v*; **oxtered him,** linked arms with him and took him, 39 7.2

pad, *n*, soft saddle used by women, 51 10.2

paddock, *n*, frog, 58 1.3

pasch, pace, *n*, Easter, 7A 7.4; 7B 7.4

pickle, *v*, peck, 7A 12.2, 14.2; 7B 12.2, 14.2; **pickles,** *pres*, 22A 3.2; 22B 2.2

pin, *n*, door knocker, rod, 53 1.3; 54 1.3

pine, *n*, pain, suffering inflicted as punishment 7A 24.4, 7B 25.4

pith, *n*, soft interior column in a stem, such as a reed, 25A 1.2; 25B 2.2

plaidie, *n*, outer garment consisting of a rectangular length of woollen cloth, 46 2.2

play, *n*; **play was played, pl'ayed,** bout or game was over, 1A 18.3; 1B 19.3

pow, *n*, head, crown of the head, 38 10.4

preens, *n pl*, pins, 3A 14.2; 3B 13.2

prinned, preened, *v pt*, pinned, 5A 13.3; 5B 13.3; 21A 7.3; 21B 7.3

pued, *v*, pulled, 4A 2.2; 4B 2.2; 20A 8.1, 11.1; 20B 6.1, 9.1

puir, *adj*, poor, 41 8.2

put, *v*; **put she on,** she got dressed, 18A 24.2; 18B 21.2

pykan, *adj*, tasty, 40 1.3 (cf. *SND* **pickant**)

quo, quo', *v pt*, said, 51 13.2, 15.1; 58 1.3

rantin', rantin, *adj*, merry, exuberant, riotous, rakish, 6A 1.4, 13.4; 6B 1.4, 13.4

rase, *v pt*, rose, 2B 4.1, 4.3; 18A 24.1; 18B 21.1 etc.

reek, *n*, smoke, 41 1.2

reek, *v*, smoke, 41 12.2

repair, *v*, go, 11B 1.4

ried, *adj*, red, 2B 3.3; 9B 9.3, 10.1 etc.

riffie o', *adj*, rich in, 39 1.2

rive, *v*, break up, 1A 10.4; 1B 11.4

rude, *n*, cross of Christ, 21A 5.1; 21B 5.1, 12.1

Sabbathday, *n*, Sunday, 1A 20.1; 1B 20.1

saddle bow, saiddle bow, *n*, pommel, arched front part of saddle, 4A 6.1; 4B 8.1; 7A 6.1

sair, *v*, serve, 21A 4.3, 11.3; 21B 3.3, 11.3; 41 5.2

sall, *v*, shall, 2A 11.3; 2B 11.3, 11.4; 9A 12.4 etc.

sanna, *v neg*, shall not, 7A 13.1, 15.1; 7B 13.1, 15.1; 51 13.4

saut, *adj*, salt, 1A 1.4, 23.2; 1B 1.4; 23B 2.4

scorn, *n*; **gies him the scorn,** mocks him, 38 9.2

screen, *n*, shawl, head-scarf, 5B 17.3

scrogs, scroggs, *n*, stunted bushes, 13A 10.2; 13B 10.2;

scuddin, *v pres p*, moving quickly, 51 12.2

see-na, *v neg*, do you not see, 38 9.1

sene syne, see **synsyne**

shapit, shappit, *v pt*, shaped, cut to pattern, 7A 7.3; 7B 7.3

shoon, *n*, shoes, 1A 18.2, 22.2; 1B 19.2, 24.2; 36 8.4 etc.

sic, siccan, *adj*, such, of such a kind, 7A 13.2, 15.2; 7B 13.2, 15.2; 23B 3.4 etc.

sillar, *n*, silver, money, 39 1.2, 2.2; 41 6.3 etc.; **siller,** *adj*, 54 1.3

silly, *adj*, simple, simple-minded, 13A 9.1, 9.2; 13B 9.1, 9.2; 46 2.3

sin, *prep*, since, 2A 8.4; 7A 17.2; 7B 17.2

sist, *v*, stop by judicial decree, 19B note

slocken, *v*, extinguish, quench, 9A 16.4; 9B 16.4

smootrekin, *adj*, tiny and active, 38 5.2

sneeshen, sneeshin, *n*, snuff, 38 4.3; 39 3.3

snood, *n*, ribbon tied round the forehead and under the hair at the back of the neck, worn by unmarried women, 5A 18.3; 5B 18.3

socht, sought, *v pt*, searched, 16A 5.1, 16B 5. 1

soomed, *v pt*, swam, 1A 18.4; 1B 19.4

sou, *n*, pig, 38 11.4

soud, sud, s'ud, suld, *v pt*, should, 2B 10.4; 6B 6.2; 19B 3.4; 30 4.1etc.

souter, soutar, sutor, *n*, shoemaker, 3A 2.3; 3B 2.3; 47 1.1

spark, *n*, young man, 51 5.1

spauld, *n*, shoulder, 21A 6.3; 21B 6.3

speul, speal, *n*, probably corruption of **scale,** shallow drinking-bowl, 3A 6.1, 7.1; 3B 6.1, 7.1

spieled, *v pt*, climbed, 51 11.1

spier, speer, *v*, ask, enquire, ask in marriage, 38 1.4; 41 2.4; 51 17.1

stan', ** *v*; **stan' aboot, stand back, 37 1.5, 2.7, 3.7 etc.

stap, *v*, step, 51 16.1

steer, *n*, helm, 1A 12.2,13.2; 1B 13.2, 14.2

stock, *n*, log, tree-stump, 51 11.3

stown, *v pp*, stolen, 6A 2.4; 6B 2.4

strae, *n*, straw, 51 3.1

studie, *n*, anvil, 25A 1.1; 25B 2.1

sweer, *adj*, reluctant, unwilling, 2A 4.2; 2B 4.2

swoor, *v pt*, swore, 39 1.4

syne, *adv*, then, afterwards, 36 11.1

synsyne, sene syne, *adv*, from that time, since then, 16A 2.4; 16B 2.4

tane, taen, ta'en, *v pp*, taken, 4A 6.4; 4B 8.4; 6A 1.3; 6B 1.3; 10A 9.4; 10B 9.4 etc.

tent, *v*, pay attention, 41 6.1

thae, *adj*, those, these 7B 24.3; 29B 3.1

think lang, *v*, weary, long, 7A   10.4; 7B   10.4; **thocht, thoucht lang,** *pt*, 25A 2.2; 25B 3.2

thrang, *n*, crowd, 2A 5.3; 2B 5.3

thraw, *v*, twist, wrench, 7B 15.3

till, *prep*, for, 2B 18.4

timmer, *adj*, wooden, 39 6.3

tine, tyne, *v*, lose, 41 7.4; 51 6.4

tippet, *v pt*, tipped, paid, rewarded, 36 3.2

tirled, *v pt*, rattled, 53 1.3

to, *prep*, for, 2A 10.1, 10.2, 10.3; 2B 10.1, 10.2, 10.3 etc.

tocher, *n*, dowry, marriage-settlement, 20A 12.4, 20B 10.4; 27A 1.4; **tocher gude**, property given as a dowry, 15A 5.2; 15B 5.2

tod, *n*, fox, 40 1.1, 2.1, 4.1; **tods,** *pl*, 40 1.2; **tod hole,** *n*, fox-hole, 40 4.1

toom, *adj*, empty, 41 10.4

toun, toon, town, *n*, town, farm, habitation, 2A 13.4; 2B 13.4; 4A 5.2, 5.4; 4B 7.2, 7.4 etc.;

tour, *n*, tower, 10A 14.1; **tours,** *pl*, 14A 4.3; 14B 4.3; 19B 4.2

towmont, *n*, twelve months, year, 20A 5.3

travise, travis, *n*, stall in a stable, 18A 23.3; 18B 20.3

tree, *n*, gallows-tree, gallows, 16A 10.4; 16B 10.4

trig, *adj*, neat, 22A 4.2; 22B 4.2

trip, *v*, move light-footedly, 42 1.2, 6.2; **trippin, trippin',** *pres p,* 8A 3.2; 8B 3.2

trow, *v*, believe, 37 1.1, 2.1, 3.1 etc.

twal, twall, *adj*, twelve, 37 1.3; 51 16.4

unco, *adj*, strange, otherworldly, unknown, 3A 5.3, 9.3; 3B 9.3; *adv*, very, 38 2.3

unkind, *adj*, unnaturally cruel, 10B 10.2

vauntie, *adj*, proud, 39 2.4

wa', *n,* wall, 2A 1.1; 2B 1.1; 3A 1.4; 3B 1.4; 6A 10.1; 6B 10.1 etc.; **wa's,** *pl,* 6A 9.3, 11.3; 6B 8.5, 11.5; 14A 7.3; 14B 7.3 etc.

wad, w'ad, wald, *v pt*, would, 1A 5.3; 1B 5.3; 2A 4.4; 2B 4.4; 7A 16.4; 7B 16.4 etc.; **wadna,** *neg*, 7A 23.1; 7B 24.1

wade, wad, *v*, wager, 6A 10.3; 6B 10.3; 9A 2.2, 2.3; 9B 2.2, 2.3 etc.

wae, *adj*, sad, distressed, 13A 3.2; 13B 3.2

wae, *n*; **wae betide**, a curse upon, 7B 11.3; 9B 7.1, 19.1; **waes,** devil is, 38 11.3

waes me, *interj*, alas, 19A 4.1, 5.1; 19B 3.1, 4.1

waft, *n*, weft, 11A 8.4, 14.4; 11B 7.4, 11.4

wait on, *v*, attend, look after, 15A 5.4; 15B 5.4

waled, *v pp*, chosen, 21A 1.3; 21B 1.3

want, *v*, lack, 13A 4.1; 35 4.4; 41 5.4

wark, *n*, work, 51 2.3

warks, *v pres*, works, 27 2.3

warn, warnin', *n*, warrant, security, safeguard, 15A 2.4, 6.4; 15B 2.4, 6.4

wasna, was-na, *v neg*, was not, 7B 21.3, 22.3

wast, *n*, west, 9B 16.3, 17.3; 13B 6.1; 21A 1.1; 21B 1.1 etc.

wat, *v*, know; **I wat,** indeed, truly, certainly, 2A 3.2, 4.2, 7.2; 2B 3.2, 4.2, 7.2 etc.

watch, *v*, keep vigil at, 2A 8.1, 9.1; 2B 8.1, 9.1

wattit, *v pp*, welted, 47 1.3

waur, *v pt*, were, 1B 19.1; 2B 9.2; 4B 1.4 etc.; **waurna,** *neg*, 14A 10.2; 14B 11.2; 15B 8.1

wee, *adj*, little, 16A 3.3, 5.3; 16B 3.3, 5.3; 38 5.1 etc.

wee, *n*; **a wee, a-wee,** a little while, 41 1.1, 3.1

weet, *n*, rain, 1A 8.3; 1B 6.3, 9.3

weet, *v*, wet, soak, 1A 18.2; 1B 19.2; 23B 2.4; **weet, wat,** *pt*, 14A 5.4; 14B 5.4

wether, wither, *n*, castrated ram, 21A 7.1, 8.3; 21B 7.1, 8.3

whaur, whare, *adv*, where, 1A 1.3, 12.1; 1B 1.3, 13.1; 2B 1.3 etc.

wheesht, *interj*, be quiet, 50 note; 51 13.2

whilk, *pron*, which, 15B note on air; 18B 8.2

whittlegait, see under **dominie**

whottle, *n*, knife, 39 3.2

wife, *n*, woman, 51 4.3, 9.1

win, *v*, get, earn, 7A 24.2; 7B 25.2; 14A 5.2; 36 6.2 etc.; **win up,** rise up, stand up, 2A 3.1; 2B 3.1; 18A 23.1; 18B 20.1

winked, *v pt*, blinked, 34 1.2

winna, wilna, *v neg*, will not, 4A 3.1; 4B 3.1; 7A 13.1; 7B 13.1; 17A 7.1; 17B 6.1 etc.

wish, wis', *v*, hope, suspect, 18A 9.2, 12.2; 18B 9.2, 11.2; 40 3.3

wishes, *n pl*, curses, 11A 5.1

woo, *n*, wool, 28 4.1

wracht, *v pp*, wrought, done, 51 2.3

wrang, *adj*, deranged, demented, 38 11.3

wude, wode, *n*, wood, 21A 12.1; 21B title

yestreen, yestre'en, *n*, yesterday evening, 1A 7.1; 1B 8.1; 16A 8.1; 16B 8.1, 10.1

yetts, *n*, gates, 15A 3.2, 3.3; 15B 3.2, 3.3

INDEX OF PEOPLE AND PLACES

The numbers of the song texts received from people mentioned are shown in bold.

Benonie; Binonie 171, 195, 199, 201
Benothie; Benothy; Bennochie 142, 186, 190, 199-200
Bethelnie 46-7, 180, 217
Bethune (Behune), Mary (Marie) 88-9
Birds; Burds; Bird family 142, 186, 190, 199-200
Bissats 142, 190
Blackwood, John xxiii
Blackwoods xxii
Blairgowrie xviii, xxxiii, 109, 111, 185
Bond, W. H. xxxi
Border, the 161, 193
Borry xxxiv, 150
Brackley 204
Braemar; Brae Mar 84-5
Brechin xxxii, xxxiv,153, 203-4
Brewster, James 203
Bridgewater; Bridge Water 38, 40
Britain xxii, xxvii-ix
Brod, Johnnie 51, 72-7, 180, 182, 199-201
Bronson, B. H. xxxviii; *passim* in the Notes at 177-97
Broughty (Brochty, Brochtie) Wa's (Walls, halls) 78-9, 82-3, 183
    199, 206-10, 212, 217
Brown, Mrs (née Anna Gordon) vii, 178
Buchan, David 187
Buchan, Peter vii, xxvi, 203-13, 217
Burns, Robert 192
Burnside, Mrs Janet xxxiii
California xxxviii
Campbell, Katherine vii-viii
Campbell, William viii
Canada xxxii
Caputh 109, 185
Carmichael, Mary (Marie) 88-9
Chambers, Robert xxi-ii
Chesnutt, Michael vii
Child, Francis James *passim*
Christie, William 196
Cluny Castle 111
Cluny, Laird of; Cluny. See under Ogilvy.
Clyde 98-9
Clydeswater; Clydes water; Clydiswater 39-43

40: 151f, **42**: 156f, **43**: 158, **50**: 161f, **52**: 165f, **53**: 170, **54**: 171, **55**: 172, **57**: 174, **58**: 175, **59**: 176

Harris, Jane *passim*

Harris, Mary xxxii

Harris, Mrs David. See under Grace Harris.

Harris, William xxxii

Hazelan. See under Glenhazlen.

Helen; Hellen; Ellen 78-83, 183, 199-201, 206-7

Henry (Henerie) V (Fifth), King 139, 141, 189-190, 216

Hind Horn 179

Hunglen 78-9, 212

Hunting, Young 38-9, 180, 216

Hurwitz, Robert xxxviii

Hustan (Huston, Houston), Molly (Mary) 156-8, 192, 200

Illinois 178

Invercauld 199

Inverness xxiii

Inverwharity 159, 193

Isabel, Lady 122-3, 187, 215

Isabell 144-5

Isdale, Mrs **26**: xxxiv-v, 129

James the Rose, Sir 189

Janet 12-17, 20-1, 112-3, 117, 186-7

Jean 162

Jean, Miss 151

Jean o Bethelnie 46-7, 180, 217

Jervise, Andrew 164, 194

Joan 191

John 28-33, 194

John, Lord 98-105

Johnnie 151

Keith, Alexander 182

Kildrummy 204

Kinalty; Kinaltie; Kinatie 82-5

Kinghorn xxi, 10-11

Kirkwall xviii

Kittredge, George Lyman xxx

La Hogue xxxviii, 165-6, 194, 200

Laing, Alexander, Brechin 203-5, 211, 213

Laing, Alexander, Newburgh xxiv

Laing, David xxi, xxvi

237

Molison, Mrs xxxiv-v, **35**: 144f; **36**: 146f
Morningside xxxii, xxxiv
Morris, Rob 47, 180
Morrison, Peggy vii
Mosey; Mosy; Mossie xxxv, 143, 190, 200
Motherwell, William xxviii
Muirton 82-5, 184
Nairn, Water 82-5
Nellie; Nelly 84-5
Newburgh xvii, xix xxiii-xxv, xxvii, xxxi-ii
Newington xxxiii
Newton Castle 111
Nile xxxv, 200-1
Norawa; Norraway 4-5
Norfolk, Duke of 179
North Carolina 179
Nygard, Holger 187
Ogilvie, Johnnie 159, 193, 199
Ogilvy, Jeanie 108-9
Ogilvy, Laird of Cluny xviii, 108-9, 111, 185
Oregon viii, xxxviii
Orkney xvii-viii
Orlange Hill 14-5
Perth xxxv
Perthshire xxxiii, 109, 178
Peterhead 203
Pitcairn Wa's; Pitcairn's Wa's 34-6
Primrose Hill xxviii
Reedin; Riedan; Rieden 38-47, 180, 199-200
Revel, Lord xxxv, 144-5, 191
Ritchie, James 111
Rob Roy xxxv, 128-9, 188, 204, 217
Robert, Prince xxxv, 146, 191, 216
Robin xxviii, xxxi, 116-21, 186-7, 191, 199-200
Robin Oigg 129
Rosemount 109
Roslyn (Roslin, Roslen), Earl o' 62-3, 181, 199-201
Roudesdales; Rudesdale; Rudiesdale; Redesdale 50-5, 180, 199-200,
    217
Royan, Nicola viii
Russel; Russell 165, 168, 201

INDEX OF TITLES AND FIRST LINES

All forms of the titles of songs, poems and tunes are included in this index, with the titles of song texts being given in capitals. The song number for each text is shown in bold and is followed, after a colon, by a reference to the full text, which is given in the style "26f" to accommodate cases where a specific version referred to is to be found on a sequence of alternate pages. In the case of first lines, where there are parallel texts and their first lines do not differ substantively, only one version is listed.

LADY O' ARNGOSK, THE **26A**: 128, 188
Lady of Arngosk, The (Child 224) 188
Lady stude in her bour door, The 38-9, 180
Laird o Logie, The (Child 182) 32-3, 179, 217
Laird o' Meldrum and Peggy Douglas, The 193
Lamkin (Child 93) xxxv, 142, 190, 216
Landlady, count the lawin 193
Lang cravat, A xxxv, 201
Langer that the ploom tree stands, The 188
Late at night 199, 201
Late at night, there I spied 156
Lord Lovel (Child 75) 144, 191, 216
LORD REVEL xxxv, **35**: 144f, 191
Lord Revel he stands in his Stable door 144
MARIE HAMILTON **16B**: 87f, 184, 199-200
MARY HAMILTON (Child 173) **16A**: 86f, 184, 216
Mary Houston 192
Mary Huston 200
Merry Wooing of Robin and Joan, the West-Country Lovers, The
    191
MOLLY HUSTAN **42**: 156f, 192
Monie a time have I and my brown foal 122
Mony a time I rade wi my broun foal 123
MOSEY, MARE xxxv, **34**: 143, 190
Mosey was a little man, a clever mare did buy 143
Mossie and His Meer 190
Mossie was a clever man 200
Mosy was a clever man 200
My father was as great a Lord 90
My husband built 201
My husband built &c 199
My husband built for me a bower 91, 184
My Love she lives 200
My love she lives in Linco'n shire 205
My Luve she lives &c 199
MY LUVE SHE LIVES IN LINCOLNSHIRE **4B**: 23f, 178, 208
My Maidens fair, yoursels prepare 137
My Mother was a proud, proud woman 86-7
My Rolling Eye xxxv
Nae Dominie/dominie for me xxxv, 200-1
Nae Dominie's for me, laddie xxxv

SIR COLIN xxxvi, **2A, B**: 12f, 177, 199, 201
Sir Collin 200
Sir James the Rose 189
Sir Patrick 201
SIR PATRICK SPENS (Child 58) xv, xix-xxii, **1A, B**: 3, 4f, 177,
    199-200, 215
Sma' Caiterin, The xxxv, 199
Soldier Lad, The xxxv
SWEET WILLIAM **17A, B**: 90f, 184, 196, 200, 209
Sweet William's Ghost (Child 77) 170, 195, 216
SWEET WILLIE **4A**: 22f, 178
TEEDLE ELL O **22A**: 120f, 187
Teem Wa's, The 192
There cam a Ghaist 200
THERE CAM A GHOST xxxix, **53**: 170, 195, 199
There cam a Ghost to Margit's door 170
There cam a knicht to Archerdale 18-9
There lived [a] farmer in the north 162
There lived a lady in the North 112-3
There lived a man, in the north west land 56-7
THERE WAUR AUCHT AN' FORTY NOBLES **8B**: 47f, 180
There waur aucht and forty nobles 46
THERE WAUR THREE LADIES **5B**: 27f, 179, 199, 201
There waur three Ladies in a ha' 27, 179
THERE WE LEFT HER **59**: 176, 197, 201
THERE WERE THREE LADIES **5A** 26f, 179, 200
There were three Ladies in a ha' 26
THERE S BUCKIES I' BOG, THERE'S GAIRIES I' GLEN **48**:
    161, 193
THEY CA' ME NELLY DOUGLAS BUTT THE HOOSE **46**:
    160, 193
TOD LOWRIE xl, **40**: 151f, 192, 199, 201
Tod lowrie's come 200
Tods wife is lyin' sick, The 152
Tutti taitie 199
Tutti tette 200
Twa Sisters, The (Child 10) 171, 195, 215
Twas Monday in the Morning the nineteenth of May 165
Wearie's Well 199
WEARIE'S WELLS **23B**: 123f , 187
WEARIES WELLS **23A**: 122f, 187

BIBLIOGRAPHY

Anderson, F. G. and Pettitt, T. 1979. "Mrs Brown of Falkland: A Singer of Tales?". *Journal of American Folklore* 92, 1-24.

Anon. 1871. *The Ballad Minstrelsy of Scotland: Romantic and Historical.* London: Bell and Daldy.

—— n.d. *A' Chòisir-Chiùil: The St. Columba Collection of Gaelic Songs.* London and Glasgow: Bayley and Ferguson.

Aytoun, W. E., ed., 1858. *The Ballads of Scotland.* 2nd edn 1859. Edinburgh: William Blackwood.

Barry, P. 1909. "Irish 'Come-all-ye's''. *Journal of American Folklore* 22, 374-88

Bronson, B. H. 1942-3. "Professor Child's Ballad Tunes". *California Folklore Quarterly* 1, 185-200.

—— 1959-72. *The Traditional Tunes of the Child Ballads.* 4 vols. Princeton: Princeton University Press.

—— 1969. "Mrs Brown and the Ballad" in *The Ballad as Song,* 64-78. Berkeley and Los Angeles: University of California Press.

Buchan, D. 1970. "Lady Isabel and the Whipping Boy". *Southern Folklore Quarterly* 34, 62-70.

—— 1972. *The Ballad and the Folk.* London: Routledge. Reprint Tuckwell Press, East Linton, 1994.

Buchan, P. 1828. *Ancient Ballads and Songs of the North of Scotland, hitherto unpublished.* 2 vols. Edinburgh: W. & D. Laing and J. Stevenson.

Chambers, R. 1859. *The Romantic Scottish Ballads: Their Epoch and Authorship.* London and Edinburgh: William and Robert Chambers.

Chappell, W. 1859. *Popular Music of the Olden Time.* London: Chappell and Co.

Child, F. J. 1882-98. *The English and Scottish Popular Ballads.* 5 vols. Boston: Houghton, Mifflin and Company. Reprinted Dover Books, New York, 1965.

Christie, W. 1876-81. *Traditional Ballad Airs.* Edinburgh: Edmonston and Douglas.

Clyne, N. 1859. *The Romantic Scottish Ballads and the Lady Wardlaw Heresy.* Limited edition. Aberdeen: A. Brown. Reprinted Norwood editions, Norwood, Pa., 1974.

—— 1863. *Ballads from Scottish History.* Edinburgh: Edmonston and Douglas.

Cowan, E. J., ed., 1980. *The People's Past.* Edinburgh: Polygon.

Day, W. G., ed., 1987. *The Pepys Ballads Catalogue of the Pepys Library at Magdalene College, Cambridge*. Cambridge: Brewer.

Edinburgh and Leith Post Office Directory. 1874-5.

Edinburgh Post Office Directory. 1873.

Firth, C. H. 1908. *Naval Songs and Ballads*. London: Navy Records Society.

Ford, R. 1904. *Vagabond Songs and Ballads,* Paisley: Alexander Gardner.

Gammack, J., ed., 1882. *The History and Traditions of the Land of the Lindsays in Angus by Andrew Jervise*. 2nd edn. Edinburgh: David Douglas.

Hales, J. W. and Furnivall, F. J., eds, 1868. *Bishop Percy's Folio MS: Ballads and Romances*. 3 vols. London: N. Trübner.

Harris, D. 1845. "The Parish of Fearn" in *The New Statistical Account of Scotland*, 11.311-20. Edinburgh and London: William Blackwood and Sons.

Hecht, H. 1904. *Songs from David Herd's Manuscripts*. Edinburgh: William J. Hay.

Henderson, H. 1980, "The Ballad, The Folk and The Oral Tradition" in Cowan 1980, 65-101.

Herd, D. 1776. *Ancient and Modern Scottish Songs, Heroic Ballads, etc.* Edinburgh: James Dickson and Charles Elliot.

Jervise, A. 1853. *The History and Traditions of the Land of the Lindsays in Angus and Mearns, with notices of Alyth and Meigle.* Edinburgh: Sutherland and Knox.

Johnson, J. 1787-1803. *The Scots Musical Museum*. 6 vols. Edinburgh: James Johnson.

Kinsley, J., ed., 1968. *The Poems and Songs of Robert Burns*. 3 vols. Oxford: Clarendon Press.

Laing, A. 1822. *Scarce Ancient Ballads, many never before published.* Aberdeen: printed for and sold by Alex. Laing.

———— 1823. *The Thistle of Scotland: A Selection of Ancient Ballads.* Aberdeen: printed for the author by J. Booth, Jun.

———— 1827. *Archie Allan; A Tale, In Scottish Verse.* Brechin: A. Black.

———— 1857. *Wayside Flowers: being Poems and Songs.* 3rd edn. Glasgow, Edinburgh and London: Blackie and Son

Low, D. A., ed., 1993. *The Songs of Robert Burns*. London: Routledge.

Lyle, E. B. 1977. "Child's Scottish Harvest". *Harvard Library Bulletin* 25, 125-54.

MacDonald, J. A. R. 1899. *The History of Blairgowrie*. Blairgowrie: The Advertiser Office.

Opie, I. and P. 1951. *The Oxford Dictionary of Nursery Rhymes*. Oxford: Clarendon Press.

Ord, J. 1930. *The Bothy Songs & Ballads of Aberdeen, Banff & Moray, Angus and the Mearns*. Paisley: A. Gardner. Reprint John Donald, Edinburgh, 1990.

Playford, J. 1651. *The English Dancing Master*. Reprint Schott, London, 1957.

Psalmodia Evangelica. 1789. London

Psalms and Hymn Tunes Selected for the Use of the Hollis-Street Society 1811. Boston.

Reppert, J. D. 1953. "F. J. Child and the Ballad", containing a list of 1,104 items of correspondence between Child and Macmath. PhD thesis, Harvard University. (Copy in Scottish Studies Library, University of Edinburgh.)

Scott, H. 1915-25. *Fasti Ecclesiae Scoticanae*. New edn. 5 vols. Edinburgh: Oliver and Boyd.

Shuldham-Shaw, P., Lyle, E. B., et al. eds, 1981-2002. *The Greig-Duncan Folk Song Collection*. 8 vols. Aberdeen: Aberdeen University Press, and Edinburgh: Mercat Press.

Struthers, J. 1819. *The Harp of Caledonia*. 2 vols. Glasgow. Edward Khull and Co.

Tans'ur, W. 1735. *A Compleat Melody*. London: W. Pearson for James Hodges.

Reid, A. 1906-11. "Psalmody Rhymes". *Miscellanea of the Rymour Club* 1, 33-8.

Warden, A. J. 1880-5. 5 vols. *Angus or Forfarshire, the Land and People*. Dundee: Charles Alexander and Co.

Watkins, J. H. 1868. "Early Scottish Ballads". *Transactions of the Glasgow Archaeological Society* 5, 438-85.

Scottish Text Society Publications

The following is a complete list of the Society's publications in print.

BS indicates that a volume is available from:

> Booksource
> 32 Finlas Street
> Cowlairs Estate
> Glasgow   G22 5DU
>
> Tel: 0141 558 1366 Fax: 0141 557 0189

STS indicates that a volume is available from:

> The Editorial Secretary
> The Scottish Text Society
> School of English Studies
> University of Nottingham
> Nottingham NG7 2RD
> e-mail: nicola.royan@nottingham.ac.uk

Prices: Where two prices are stated the figure in brackets applies to non-members. Unless otherwise stated volumes are £30 each to non-members. Annual Subscription rates are £20 for individuals and £30 for institutions. All prices include postage and packing.

Please note that members of the Society should order back copies from the Secretary at the address above. Volumes are new and bound unless otherwise stated. Only a handful of copies remain in the First, Second and Third Series. Would-be purchasers are advised not to delay in securing their copies.

FIRST SERIES

1884-85   5 *Leslie's Historie of Scotland* **I** Ed. E G Cody.
STS   (1 Second hand Copy). £20

1885-86   7 *Schir William Wallace* **II** (See 6 above).
STS   (3 Unbound Copies). £6 (£12)

1903-04 52 *The New Testament in Scots* **III** (See 46, 49 above).
STS   (4 Unbound Copies.) £6 (£12)

1905-06 56 *The Original Chronicle of Andrew of Wyntoun* **V** Fourth
volume of text. (See 50, 53, 54 above).
BS

1908-09 62 *Gilbert of the Haye's Prose MS (1456)* **II** *The Buke of the Ordre of Knychthede* and *The Buke of the Governaunce of Princis* (See 44 above).
STS (8 Copies) £20 (2 Unbound Copies) £6 (£12)

SECOND SERIES

1919-20 10 *Habakkuk Bisset's Rolment of Courtis* **I** Ed. P J Hamilton-Grierson.
STS (1 Second hand Copy). £20

12 *The Buik of Alexander* **II** Ed. R L Graeme Ritchie.
STS (1 Unbound Copy) £6 (£12)

1921-22 13 *Habakkuk Bisset's Rolment of Courtis* **II** (See 10 above).
STS (2 Second hand Copies). £20 (1 Unbound Copies.) £6 (£12)

1929-30 26 *The Bannatyne Manuscript* **IV** (See 22, 23 above).
STS (1 Second hand Copy). £20

THIRD SERIES

1939-40 14 *Thomas Hudson's Historie of Judith* Ed. James Craigie.
STS (5 Copies). £20

FOURTH SERIES

1965 2 *The Meroure of Wysdome by Johannes de Irlandia* **II** (See Second Series 19 above). Ed. F Quinn.
BS ISBN 0 9500245 7 0

1968 4 *Hary's Wallace* **I** Ed. Matthew P McDiarmid.
BS ISBN 0 9500245 0 3

1969 5 *Hary's Wallace* **II** (See 4 above).
BS ISBN 0 9500245 8 9

1970 6 *The Works of Allan Ramsay* **IV** (See Third Series 19, 20, 29: same editors as 29).
BS ISBN 0 9500245 1 1

1972 7 *The Works of Allan Ramsay* **V** (See 6 above and Third Series 19, 20, 29 above: same editors as 6).
BS ISBN 0 9500245 2 X

1974 8 *The Works of Allan Ramsay* **VI** (See 6, 7 above and Third Series 19, 20, 29 above: same editors as 7).

BS   ISBN 0 9500245 3 8

1975   9 *Andrew Crawfurd's Collection of Ballads and Songs* I Ed. E B Lyle.
　　　　　BS   ISBN 0 9500245 4 6

1977   10 *James Watson's Choice Collection* I Ed. Harriet Harvey Wood.
　　　　　BS   ISBN 0 9500245 5 4

1979   11 *The Complaynt of Scotland* Ed. A M Stewart.
　　　　　BS   ISBN 0 9500245 9 7

1981   13 *Barbour's Bruce* III Text of Books XI-XX. (See 12 above).
　　　　　BS   ISBN 1 897976 01 1

1984   15 *Barbour's Bruce* I Introduction, notes and glossary. (See 12, 13 above). (Published 1985).
　　　　　BS   ISBN 1 897976 02 X

1985   16 *The Buik of King Alexander the Conqueror* II Ed. John Cartwright. Lines 1 to 9268. (Published 1986).
　　　　　BS   ISBN 1 897976 03 8

1986   17 *Selected Sermons of Zachary Boyd* Ed. David W Atkinson. (Published 1989).
　　　　　BS   ISBN 1 897976 04 6

1987   18 *The Buik of King Alexander the Conqueror* III Lines 9269 to end. (See 16 above). (Published 1990).
　　　　　BS   ISBN 1 897976 05 4

1988   19 *The Meroure of Wysdome by Johannes de Irlandia* III Ed. Craig McDonald. (See Second Series 19, Fourth Series 2 above). (Published 1990).
　　　　　BS   ISBN 1 897976 06 2

1989   20 *James Watson's Choice Collection* II (See 10 above). (Published 1991).
　　　　　BS   ISBN 1 897976 07 0

1990   21 *The Prose Works of Sir Gilbert Hay* III *The Buke of the Ordre of Knychthede* and *The Buke of the Gouernaunce of Princis* Ed. Jonathan Glenn. (Published 1993).
　　　　　BS   ISBN 1 897976 08 9

1991   22 *The Deidis of Armorie* I Ed. Luuk Houwen. Text, textual notes and bibliography. (Published 1995).
　　　　　BS   ISBN 1 897976 09 7

1992   23 *The Deidis of Armorie* II Commentary, glossary and appendices. (See 22 above). (Published 1995).

BS ISBN 1 897 976 10 0

1993   24 *Andrew Crawfurd's Collection of Ballads and Songs* **II** Ed. E B
Lyle. (See 9 above). (Published 1996).
BS ISBN 1 897976 11 9

1994   25 *David Hume of Godscroft's History of the House of Douglas* **I**
Ed. David Reid. (Published 1996).
BS ISBN 1 897976 12 7

1995   26 *David Hume of Godscroft's History of the House of Douglas* **II**
Ed. David Reid. (See 25 above). (Published 1996).
BS ISBN 1 897976 13 5

1996   27 *The Buke of the Chess* Ed. Catherine van Buuren. (Published
1998).
BS ISBN 1 897976 14 3

1997   28 *The Poems of Alexander Montgomerie* **I** Ed. David J Parkinson.
(Published 2000).
BS ISBN 1 897976 15 1

1998   29 *The Poems of Alexander Montgomerie* **II** Ed. David J
Parkinson. (Published 2000).
BS ISBN 1 897976 16 X

1999   30 *The Song Repertoire of Amelia and Jane Harris* Ed. Emily Lyle,
Kaye McAlpine and Anne Dhu Lucas (Published 2002).
BS ISBN 1 897976 17 8